BIBLICAL STRATEGIES FOR A COMMUNITY IN CRISIS

What African Americans Can Do

Dr. Colleen Birchett,
Editor

A **umi** Publication
urban ministries, inc.
Chicago, IL 60643

Publisher
Urban Ministries, Inc.
1350 West 103rd Street
Chicago, Illinois 60643
(312) 233-4499

First Edition
First Printing
ISBN: 0-940955-19-9
Catalog No. 2-2734

Scripture quotations are from the King James Version of the Bible unless otherwise stated. Printed in the United States of America.

DEDICATION

This book is dedicated to all of the ministers and pastors whom God has used to make a lasting impact on my life and in the lives of members of my family.

CONTENTS

ACKNOWLEDGMENTS

We wish to acknowledge the outstanding contributions of publications manager and designer, Shawan Brand; copy editor, Mary C. Lewis; and word processors Sara Hennings and Caron B. Davis, without whose help the book could not have come into existence. Last, but not least, we wish to thank Media Graphics Corporation and Dickinson Press.

PREFACE

Dr. Colleen Birchett

The title of this book, "Biblical Strategies for a Community in Crisis" is one that might attract the attention of a cross-section of people representing a wide variety of backgrounds. However, there are two facts about which most people would agree: 1) The African American community is in a state of crisis. 2) The Bible has a message of hope that relates to this crisis.

The Bible's message of hope is the central theme of this book. The book presents the ideas of eleven influential African American leaders on the Bible's message for the African American community. Each author presents strategies for equipping the Black church to relate to the community in which it finds itself. A separate Leader's Guide illustrates how the book can be used in group study.

Private Study. Leaders might encourage participants who want to use the book as a private devotional guide, to spread the material out over weeks or perhaps months. They should be encouraged to select a different chapter each week or month. Then they might select different exercises each day until the exercises for a given chapter are exhausted.

Once all of the chapters are completed, the leader might encourage participants to read additional books and periodical articles from the bibliography at the end of the book. These books can be used to extend group or private study. They provide additional information and support as the reader continues to reflect on how the Black church can serve the Black community.

Group Study — 90-Minute Sessions. The book is designed for a two-part group study session. Part I would be a time when participants, under the direction of a group leader (or minister), study Part One of the chapter, along with the "case study" presented. This initial study session would require about 30 minutes. Then the group leader would begin the "laboratory" session. In the laboratory session, the group would, collectively, investigate the Scipture presented at the end of each chapter.

The group study session is designed so that every person can contribute something to the understanding and application of the principles covered in the chapter. This process would begin as the group leader divides the larger group into five smaller groups. Each small group would be assigned a separate exercise from the set provided with the Bible study.

A small group leader would be appointed or elected for each small group. Within the small groups, the small group leader would assign one question (or two, depending on the size of the group) to each participant. In the event that there are more participants in the small group than there are questions, then people might work on questions in two's, three's or more. About ten minutes should be allowed for each small group participant to answer the question assigned to him/her. Then another ten minutes should be allowed for participants to present their answers to the small group of which they are a part. The remainder of the time should be spent allowing the small group to discuss the "summary question" which is the last question of each exercise.

At the end of the small group discussions, the smaller groups would reconvene with the larger group. In the larger group, a spokesperson from each of the five smaller groups would summarize their small group discussion. Then the larger group, under the direction of the original leader, would discuss the final "Church Based Ministry" and the "Personal Application" at the end of each chapter.

Group Study — 60-Minute Sessions. In shorter periods, it might be necessary to use part of a given chapter as a stimulus for discussion during the group meeting itself. Then the other part of the chapter might be used as a "homework" assignment or for private devotional study.

Family Devotions. During the week preceding the study of a given chapter, all members would read a given chapter privately, along with the "Bible Application" study at the end of the chapter. Each member would select a different related "discovery" exercise and, on the basis of it, prepare a short presentation for family devotions.

The devotional period would begin with a discussion of the points the author makes in the chapter. Then the "Bible Application" Scripture would be read. Each member would present their insights based on the exercise (related to the Scripture) that they read during the week. After each member has contributed, then the family, together, would discuss the "Bible Application" and "Personal Application" at the end of each chapter.

In summary, the book can be used in many ways. However, the main purpose is that African American churches everywhere become equipped to deal with critical issues currently facing Black communities, and develop a closer relationship with the Lord Jesus Christ.

INTRODUCTION

Dr. Colleen Birchett

This book goes to press at the beginning of the second year of the final decade of the 20th century. This is a pivotal moment in the history of the African American church. It is a time in which both leaders and laity are reviewing the results of data from the 1990 edition of the United States Census, to interpret its meaning for the African American community. African Americans are watching daily news programs and talk shows, and listening closely to sermons being delivered from pulpits.

As the Black community heads toward the 21st century, many people are watching the progress of the famine in Ethiopia and the political crisis in South Africa as reported through the white–controlled media. Others are noting the bombs which have ripped through many communities of African descent in various parts of the African Diaspora during the closing decades of the 20th century.

On the home front, many are taking notes on the escalation of drugs and related crimes in African American communities, and many are noting the multiplication of the HIV virus throughout Black communities. Black people are noting the rising unemployment rates, the escalating infant mortality figures, and the gradually declining life expectancy figures for African Americans (African American males, in particular).

Some are noting the reversal of many laws and amendments which were designed to protect civil rights of African Americans and other people considered "minorities" within America. Words such as "genocide" and "survival" have become a part of daily conversations. However, while many despair, African Americans who have a personal relationship with Jesus Christ realize that in Him, that is, in obedience to Him, there is hope.

This is a pivotal period for the African American church because, today as yesterday, the African American church is being

17

called upon to share hope in a world that is in crisis (Matthew 28:16-28). The African American church is being called upon to take the steps necessary to turn around the trends which threaten the survival of the Black church and the Black community as we know them today.

In this critical moment, God's people must glance behind, perhaps to this time last century, to assess where they have been. Then God's people must examine the Black community today, and the position of the Black church within that community. Then the Black church, with God as its Helper, will be in a position to chart the course for the future, and position the Black church in the Black community of the 21st century.

A Glance Behind. This time last century for African Americans, the context of the African American community was very different, yet very similar to the situation in which the community finds itself today. At that time the African American church emerged and positioned itself at the center of that community, in the center of that world.

This time last century, the abolition of slavery had issued chaos into many parts of Africa and into the lives of people of African descent throughout various parts of the Diaspora—particularly in the United States. Due to the wealth that Western countries had amassed as a result of slavery, industrializing nations were no longer based primarily on agriculture.

They had moved from agricultural economies, to mercantile economies and then on to economies based on manufacture of goods. The need for slaves was not the same anymore, and the time was ripe for the abolition of slavery. It was a time to create new relationships with the African countries from whom slaves had been acquired, and with the people they had formerly held in bondage.

However, for the most part, Western nations did not intend to base their new relationships on equality but on new forms of exploitation (Davidson, Basil, *The African Slave Trade,* p. 32).[1] While the end of slavery plunged many African countries into

18

chaos, European countries moved in to seize African land, rob it of natural resources and colonize the people.

By the 1890s, as European countries were fighting wars, and developing the political and economic machinery that carved Africa into colonies, other developments were taking place in the United States. In America, southern state governments were busily instituting and enforcing "Black Codes," "Jim Crow Laws" and other legal machinery that would continue to reverse gains made by African Americans during Reconstruction.

Reconstruction (1865-1876) had been an era in which the United States government had attempted to reconstruct southern state governments which had originally seceded from the Union over the issue of slavery and forced the country into the Civil War. To reconstruct the South, a committee of fifteen Radical Republicans had attempted to set in motion the legal framework which would: 1) rebuild the southern economy on the basis of industry, rather than slavery; 2) politically subdue the South; 3) integrate freed Africans into the mainstream of American life; and 4) protect Blacks from re-enslavement, exploitation and abuse.

To initiate this reconstruction, the Radical Republicans were successful in getting the Thirteenth Amendment and the Reconstruction Act passed. They established the Freedmen's Bureau in March, 1865, obtained relief work for former slaves, regulated labor contracts, administered justice related to Blacks, managed abandoned and confiscated lands of southern planters, and organized schools for African Americans.

However, as previously mentioned, by the 1890s a more conservative and reactionary United States Congress and judiciary, along with aggressive southern state governments were all engaged in a "backlash" against the new gains of Blacks. This backlash would reverse the gains made during Reconstruction by instituting "Black Codes," "Jim Crow Laws," sharecropping systems and terrorism. The issues around which the new conflicts revolved were the right of Blacks to vote, civil liberties of Blacks, and redistribution of land once held by southern planters.

19

Consequently, by this time last century, Black people were beginning to migrate *en masse* from rural areas of the South into southern, western, and northern cities. They had great expectations, but unfortunately, they were soon to enter a new phase of oppression and exploitation. They were to find themselves in segregated residential areas, in dilapidated, overcrowded houses. They were to become the "last hired" and the "first fired," as European immigrants poured into the cities and competed with them for low-paying jobs.

They were soon to experience poor health, high mortality rates, police brutality, and increased terrorism. Lynchings and mob violence against Blacks escalated. By the first year of the 20th century, at least 100 lynchings of Blacks had occurred. By 1914, there had been more than 1,100 (Karenga, *Introduction to Black Studies,* p. 109).[2] Very few African Americans outside of a handful of leaders could have begun to understand the complex world system against which they were fighting. Any equation that would attempt to account for the survival of African Americans during and after this period, would be inadequate unless it included the Lord, the great Liberator! The Lord brought order out of this chaos.

One of His instruments was the Black church, which had once existed as an "invisible institution" during slavery, and was a separatist Black church movement of such free Blacks as Richard Allen (founder of the African Methodist Episcopal church). From the Black church, leadership for the task of survival and empowerment emerged.

Many of the leaders the Lord used were pastors of local churches. The church became the focal point of community life. There was no division of the sacred and the secular. Even the failure of the government to provide land appears not to have crushed the African American spirit. For it was during the period following the failure of Reconstruction that the number of Black churches mushroomed, along with the growth of Black church membership.

During the final decades of the 19th century and the early decades of the 20th century, national religious organizations expanded their membership. By 1906, there were 36,770 Black churches in the United States. Of that number, 90% were located in the South. At that time, the membership in these organizations was in the neighborhood of 3,685,097 (Simms, 1926).[3] These included the African Methodist Episcopal Church, the National Baptist Convention, and others. It was a valiant struggle, and the Black church emerged victorious.

Through these churches, social services were provided for the membership and for the African American community at large. Ministries such as burial societies, benevolent societies, centers for seniors and mutual aid societies were organizations of the church. Churches formed hospitals, employment ministries, political action groups, orphanages and retirement centers. Churches also cooperated with the Freedman's Bureau and other community groups to offer tutorial programs and Christian education programs.

During this period, in response to discrimination against Black ministers in white seminaries, African American churches founded seminaries. The African Methodist Episcopal Church established Wilberforce, Payne and Turner Seminaries, and a number of smaller schools and colleges. The African Methodist Episcopal Zion Church established five colleges and academies. The Christian Methodist Episcopal Church established five colleges and lower schools. By 1926, Black churches owned and supported 153 schools, and attendance at these schools was in the range of 17,299.

It was in the late 19th century and early 20th century that such organizations as the NAACP were formed and supported by the Black Church. These groups demanded the right to justice, the vote, education, abolition of Jim Crow, equal treatment in the armed forces, and the enforcement of the 13th, 14th and 15th Amendments. During the decades following the failure of Reconstruction, the Urban League was formed and sought jobs, housing, recreation facilities and health clinics for African Americans.

Moreover, it was eleven years after the date historians mark as the failure of Reconstruction (1876), that Marcus Garvey, a Christian, was born in 1887. Garvey later organized more than a million African Americans to form the Universal Negro Improvement Association, and he began teaching people of African descent throughout the Diaspora to recognize a worldwide pattern of exploitation operating throughout the African Diaspora and in the United States. Booker T. Washington and W.E.B. DuBois also emerged during this period, teaching creative strategies for dealing with oppression. All three of these leaders were, to some extent, influenced by the Black church.

Although divided in opinion, with great ambivalence at times, and with varying levels of commitment, for the most part the Black church formed a partnership with Black community leaders to fight for civil rights of African Americans and other disenfranchised groups. This valiant struggle continued throughout the 20th century, figuring prominently in such confrontations as the Montgomery Bus Boycott which led to desegregated transportation throughout the South, and in mayoral, governmental and presidential campaigns. Eventually civil rights activities resulted in Black elected officials at every level of the United States government.

In summary, during the decades following the failure of Reconstruction, and throughout the 20th century, the Black church positioned itself at the center of the Black community and while spreading the Gospel, also worked for the elevation of the quality of life of African Americans.

An Examination of the Present. Today, more than 100 years after the failure of Reconstruction, the Black church finds itself in an African American community that has changed, as a result of dramatic victories won during the 20th century. However, the church finds itself in the midst of a community that is, in many ways, disturbingly similar to that which existed 100 years ago.

Once again, we are in the midst of a "backlash" against Black gains during the '60s and '70s. This backlash escalated during the Reagan administration and has continued with the Bush administration. The backlash initially made itself felt with the reduction of expenditures for job training, health care, affordable housing for the poor, and other cuts in domestic programs. These cuts were paired with an escalation in military expenditures and with tax cuts for the affluent, all of which created deep deficits in essential programs, and most of which affected African Americans in one way or another.

The Reagan and Bush administrations overturned important civil rights legislation. An example is the reversal of standards governing proof of discrimination that had been in effect since 1971. Another example is the limiting of nondiscrimination guarantees in the 1966 Civil Rights Act, to the hiring and not to the acts of racial harassment against employees.

Other decisions, such as *Martin vs. Wilkes,* allowed white employees to challenge affirmative action programs long after they had been instituted, but denied this same right to minorities and women wanting to challenge seniority systems with a discriminatory impact. Over 200 cases of illegal discrimination have already been dismissed as a result of Martin vs. Wilkes. The Civil Rights Act of 1990 would have overturned such decisions but was vetoed by Bush. If this trend of reversing civil rights gains continues, many if not most of the gains made during the Civil Rights Movement will be lost.

This entire scenario is disturbingly similar to a previous backlash scenario which resulted in the failure of Reconstruction at the end of the 19th century.

Moreover, as the last decade of the 20th century begins, structures are being put in place on the international scene that will result in a larger influx of immigrants from eastern Europe. This, too, is disturbingly similar to one that existed at the end of the 19th century.

The Soviet Union has recently gone out of existence, the Berlin Wall separating East and West Germany has come down, and the European Common Market has emerged. Economic and political chaos in many eastern and western European countries will cause many to leave their homes, immigrate to America, and compete for jobs sought or held by African Americans and others classified as "minorities." Both the European Common Market and the United States Immigration Service are expected to increase restrictions on the immigration of Blacks from politically and economically oppressed countries such as Haiti. Meanwhile, they are expected to encourage the immigration of whites from Eastern Europe. This is happening as famine is sweeping across many parts of Africa, and political turmoil rages in South Africa, Haiti, and Jamaica.

On the home front, even more disturbing are the current discrepancies between Black and white life expectancies. The general life expectancy for all Americans born in 1990 is projected as 75.6, with 71.4 for Blacks, 67.7 for Black males, and 75.0 for Black females.[4] Advanced data based on the 1990 census revealed that 12.6% of the white population had reached the age of 65 or older, compared to 8.1% for Blacks, 9.2 for Black women and 7.0 for Black males.[5] These figures alone would signal a discrepancy in the quality of life between Blacks and whites, and that the factors giving rise to this discrepancy are having an impact on the life span of African Americans, Black males in particular.

Another disturbing trend reflected in census data is the lack of availability of Black males to head a large percentage of Black female-headed households. The ratio of single Black women to single Black men, between the ages of 15-24, is 99 single men per 100 single women, compared to 114 single white men per 100 single white women. However, by the time the sexes reach the ages of 25-34, there are only 89 single Black men per 100 single Black females (compared to 132 single white men per 100 single white females). By the time the sexes reach 35-44, there

24

are only 67 single Black males per 100 single Black females, compared to 97 single white males for every 100 single white females.

One of the factors affecting the availability of Black men to head Black households is violence, which is reducing the overall number of men available. According to data of the 1988 National Center for Health Statistics, the number of 15-24–year–olds killed by firearms increased by 20% for African American males between 1984-1986 alone. In 1991, there were a total of 927 homicide victims in the city of Chicago alone. Of these, 703 were Blacks killing Blacks. Moreover, more than half of the 20,000 murders committed in the United States during 1991 were Black on Black offenses. In 1990, 6,591 Black males between the ages of 15-34 were killed.[6]

In fact, according to the Pediatric Trauma Registry, National Institute for Disability and Rehabilitation Research, in 1989, two percent of the children who were admitted for injuries were children suffering from gunshot wounds. This represented a 70% increase since 1986, and 40% of these shootings occurred at home.[7]

In fact, a 1989 report of the United States Department of Justice indicated that 90.8 per 1,000 Black males between the ages of 12-15, had been victims of violent crimes, whereas for Black males 16-19, it was 101 per 1,000. This can be compared to 65.7 and 89.4 per 1,000 respectively, for white males. The National Center for Health Statistics, in March, 1991, reported that 48% of Black males between the ages of 15-19 who were killed in 1988, died from gunshot wounds, compared to 18% for white males in this age range.[8]

National and local law enforcement agencies speculate that much of this violence is related to drugs. There are no accurate figures on the number of drug users in the Black community. However, in a Gallup Poll which surveyed teenagers across the United States, in response to the question of what they feel is the biggest problem facing people their age, 55% of African American teenagers felt that drug abuse itself was the biggest

25

problem, compared to 54% for white teenagers.[9] Moreover, when they were asked how serious a problem drug abuse is in their community, 39% of Black teenagers felt it was a very serious problem, compared to 27% of white teenagers.[10]

Another factor reducing the availability of Black men to head households of single Black female mothers is the spread of sexually transmitted diseases such as AIDS and syphilis. Recent statistics of the Center for Disease Control reflect that about 27% of all AIDS cases are African Americans, even though African Americans constitute only about 12% of the general American population. The CDC also reported that 90% of all AIDS cases are male, and that 75% of the males infected are between the ages of 25-40.

In summary, many other statistics could be presented here, concerning high school dropout rates, specific health conditions, etc. However, space does not permit a breakdown of statistics in that much detail.

The effects of the realities presented in these statistics already are and will continue to become more apparent in children's ministries such as Vacation Bible School, Sunday School, Bible Clubs and Scouting groups. The question is, what do they mean in terms of the content and direction of youth outreach programs in local Black churches?

The Role of the Black Church. In some form or another, the personal problems that "fall out" from the above realities will reach the doors of Black churches, either through problems confronting individual church members, or through problems in the community.

How is the Black Church positioning itself in the Black community today? Recent studies on the Black church at the end of the century seem to suggest that, while the church is still meaningful to a majority of African Americans, most churches apparently are not aware of, are ignoring, or do not understand how the grim realities reflected in these statistics, relate to their mission of world and community evangelism (Matthew 28:16-40).

In spite of today's dismal local and international realities, apparently African Americans still attend church in higher percentages than white Americans do. According to a survey of the National Research Council in Washington D.C., in 1984, 57.3% of Black Americans reported attending church, compared to 42.9% of white Americans.[11]

Some of the most revealing information about the positioning of the Black church in the Black community today is contained in a very important 1990 study by Eric Lincoln and Lawrence Mamiya. Their research has been published by Duke University in the book, *The Black Church in the African American Experience*. Lincoln and Mamiya surveyed over 2,150 Black churches to gain information on a variety of characteristics and church programs.[12]

In the Lincoln/Mamiya study, of 2,150 churches contacted, the average size of church membership was 390, with Black men constituting only 18% of the members. Black youth constituted 26% of the members. Of those enrolled in Sunday School, with an average attendance of 83, Black men comprised only 12% of that number, and Black youth comprised 58%. These data may suggest that, within the Black community, the Black church is now positioned at the center of the lives of many Black women but is not as successful in reaching Black men.[13]

In a related 1986 study, by the editor (C. Birchett) for Urban Ministries, Inc. of Chicago, published in *Urban Church Education* edited by Donald Rogers, 240 representatives of local Black churches were asked to rank the various missions of the Black church in terms of priority, 1-9. When the responses were tabulated, at the top of the list were "worship God together as a people," and "evangelize lost Blacks" (1.7 and 2.7 respectively). At the bottom of the list were "provide social services" and "organize for political action."[14] These data would seem to suggest that today's Black churches may not relate evangelism to providing social services or facilitating political empowerment, as it may have at a former time.

Support for this notion is found in other data, such as the Lincoln and Mamiya study. Of 2,150 churches contacted, 67.9%

had cooperated with social agencies and other non-church programs to deal with community problems. In urban settings the percentage was somewhat higher, at 70.9%. However, when the data are scrutinized more closely, 43.5% reported cooperating primarily with traditional civil rights organizations such as the NAACP.[15]

Only 5.3% had cooperated with employment agencies, only 2.1% had day care centers or nurseries, only 4.4% had drug and alcohol abuse agencies, and less than 8% cooperated with senior citizens or elderly agencies, welfare rights or housing programs, or police-community relations programs. Only 6.8% had food programs or clothing banks. Only 5.2% cooperated with community tutoring or educational programs.

When asked whether they allowed their church building to be used by non-church community organizations as a meeting place, 56.7% of the 2,150 churches contacted by Lincoln and Mamiya said that they did not. Of those that did, the community organization involved was most likely to be a block club (25.2%) or a traditional civil rights organization (19.1%). When asked about the nature of their community outreach programs, of the 2,150 churches contacted, 29.5% had no such programs. However, 31.5% had civil rights programs of some type.[16]

Moreover, Lincoln and Mamiya asked 1,531 clergy to list pastoral responsibilities in terms of their importance. Preaching was listed first (60%), teaching was listed second (23.4%), church administration was listed third (4.0%), and leadership of groups within the church was listed as fourth (2.5%). Civic leadership and visitation/counseling were tied at next to last, with fundraising being at the bottom.[17]

Again, the data would seem to suggest that while Black churches do cooperate with and sponsor some traditional civil rights organizations, outside of a relatively small percentage of "super churches" where such programs are common, most Black churches have not positioned themselves in the community as they did following the failure of Reconstruction. The data seem to indicate that most churches may not consider this one of their primary missions, as so many Black churches once did.

It is important to note that quite a few churches still position themselves within the Black community in ways that are very similar to those in which the Black church functioned following the failure of Reconstruction. However, the data would seem to suggest that, for most Black churches this is no longer the case.

Black Super Churches. Certain realities cannot be reflected in the data that Birchett, Mamiya or Lincoln have collected. That is, the data do not reveal the large number of "super" Black churches that are emerging throughout the country—churches where an abundance of souls are being won to the Lord, and where there are an abundance of social programs and activities designed to promote political empowerment. The data do not reflect the churches across the country which have formed the backbone of voter registration drives, and which have undergirded political campaigns that resulted in increases in voter registration and Black elected officials.

From 1970 to 1988, in addition to Reverend Jesse Jackson nearly capturing the Democratic Party nomination, the number of African Americans in national and state legislatures increased from 179 in 1970 to 424 in 1988. There was an increase of Blacks in city and county offices, from 719 in 1970 to 4,089 in 1988. The voter registration drives which helped cause these victories may not have been possible without widespread participation of Black churches.[18]

The data are not designed to relate the many positive spiritual benefits which have come to members of the Black community as a result of their decision to accept Jesus Christ as their personal Saviour. There is no way to report, in such a format, the many thousands of stories of "How I Got Over," which are the backbone of the Black church and the reason for its continued relevance within the Black community.

It is not social programs or voter registration drives which are at the core of the Black church worship experience, and it is important to note this. Whatever happens with the institutional Black church as it is known today, nothing will happen to the Spirit of the Black church regardless of the structure of its internal programs, or the condition of the building in which it is housed.

Summary: Charting the Course for the 21st Century. In charting the course for the 21st century, individual churches cannot ignore the grim realities reflected in the data presented by the United States Census Bureau and other agencies. While, due to undercounting and other problems, the data may not contain as much accuracy as would be desirable, the dramatic nature of some of it does provide the logic for taking a closer look at what is happening in the Black community today.

It demands that responsible Christians take seriously some of the trends sweeping the community. It is necessary to broaden one's view from day-to-day subsistence to a more panoramic view which takes in the past and visualizes the future, based on current realities.

The chapters which follow are largely transcripts of some of the Black church's most powerful sermons and workshop presentations of the late 20th century. They are delivered by a distinguished group of ministers and laypeople who have been intimately involved with the leadership in the Black church. Collectively, the wisdom they provide can be used as a springboard for ideas and plans for the future of the Black church.

CHAPTER ONE

It was 12:00 p.m., lunchtime at Royco's. Sadie the waitress had just taken the last order from the men of Division #9 at the tire factory, when the usual argument between them began. As usual, the debate was between the followers of Christ and the followers of Islam.

Today, Abdul interrupted Smitty as he tried to relay something that had happened at his church's prayer meeting.

"You still studying that white man's religion?" Abdul laughed.

"Why do you say it's a white man's religion?" Smitty asked.

"Well, for one thing, that Bible you study was written by, for and about white people. It has nothing to do with Black people," Abdul responded, grinning.

"That's a lie," Alfred butted in. "The Bible is written about events that took place mostly in the lives of Black people."

"Aw, Come on, man!" Abdul yelled. "Jesus was a white Jew!"

"You don't know what you're talking about," said Smitty. "Jesus was Black. You can tell from His genealogy."

"Oh, no," Sadie remarked, as she approached their table with their hamburgers. "When will you guys ever settle this argument over religion?"

> *"When you see Smitty and Alfred over at the mosque, where they belong." Abdul laughed.*
> *"He means when you see Abdul over at prayer meeting." Smitty chuckled and reached for his hamburger and fries.*

In 1989, the "New York Times" estimated that about one million of the six million Muslims in the United States were African Americans and as high as 90% of the new converts were African Americans.[1] If there really are six million people practicing Islam, Islam is the second largest religion in America, next to Christianity.[2] Lincoln and Mamiya, in their recent study of the Black church, estimated that most of the new converts to Islam are Black men (Lincoln and Mamiya, 1991).[3]

While Islam has offered many positive benefits to its converts, such as discipline, business sense, and a commitment to the Black community, the main danger that it poses in the Black community is that it has been drawing people away from a commitment to Jesus Christ as their personal Saviour. Followers of Islam assert that Christianity is a white man's religion, and that the Bible is written by, for and about white people.

In the following article, Dr. Clarence Walker addresses the issue of whether Christianity is a white man's religion by identifying the Black presence in the Bible, the sacred text which is at the heart of the Christian faith. He raises the point that most of the people who wrote and are featured in the Bible (including Jesus Christ Himself) are of African descent.

THE AFRICAN PRESENCE IN SCRIPTURE

Dr. Clarence Walker
Genesis 9:19; 10:1, 6-8, 13-20

The above passage is known as the Table of Nations. For locating the Black presence in Scripture, it is an invaluable tool. The table documents the migration of the earliest ancestors of humankind. If one were to trace these ancient migrants and their descendants through the pages of Scripture, one would discover that most of the people of the Bible were Black people.

This chapter provides an overview of some of these early migrants, along with an overview of the contributions the descendants of some of these migrants made to human civilization. It also provides an overview of some of the Black people and nations mentioned in the Bible, along with information about why knowledge of the Black presence in Scripture is important.

Personalities of the Table of Nations. In Genesis 10, the Table of Nations indicates that people of the world descended from three major patriarchs, the sons of Noah: Shem, Ham and Japheth (10:1). "Japheth" means bright, fair, wide-spreading, enlarged. Japheth came from the son of Noah and he represents the Aryan race, the Indo-Europeans, the Caucasians or white folks. Shem represents the Shemites, the Semites, or the descendants of Abraham (10:21). Then there was Ham, and the sons of Ham: Cush, Mizraim, Phut, and Canaan (10:6).[4]

Ham is the patriarch of Black folks. In fact, the name "Ham" means warm, hot and dark–skinned. The name Ham comes from the name Cam, an Egyptian word. In fact, it is the strongest term for Black. It means Black lamb or Black people. "Mizraim" means Egypt (10:6) and is the Greek name for Egyptians. However, Egyptian is not what these people called themselves. They called their land *Kemet,* and they called themselves Chem of Cam which is the strongest term in their language for Black.[5]

The Canaanites were a Black people who settled in Palestine (10:6). The name "Palestine" comes from *Paleshem,* which is related to the Philistines. The heritage of the Philistines can be traced back through Israel and Egypt. These were Black people.[6]

Misconceptions about the Black presence in Scripture can be traced to many misunderstandings of biblical events. One of the best known of these is the supposed curse of Ham (Genesis 9:22-25). The curse of Ham was actually a curse of Canaan. However, it was Noah who cursed Canaan and not God! In any case, God corrected this curse. God saw what Noah did and he took divine steps to correct it. Recall that Melchizedek, chief of Salem was a Canaanite! God has the divine audacity to tell us that Jesus Christ was a high priest after the order of Melchizedek. He corrected it.

Then the Lord had the audacity to allow four Canaanite women to enter into the blood genealogy of our Lord and Saviour Jesus Christ. In it we read of Tamah who got involved with Judah. We read of Rahab, Ruth, and Bathsheba, all of whom were Canaanites. This says something about what God thinks of the Black woman. The Black woman is all right with Him.

Cushites settled Africa (10:7). "Cush" means Black-faced. We all come from Cush. The *Unger Bible Dictionary* informs us that the Cushites migrated to Africa. Cush and Ethiopia refer to the same place. Both terms mean black face or burnt-faced people. The King James writer substituted Ethiopia instead of Cush for racist reasons. But Cushites were the folks who settled in the areas of Africa outside of Egypt. The Sudanese, or Nubians called them Christians. The Arabs called them Moors. The Europeans called them Negroes. The ancient Egyptians called them Cushites, but they were all the same folks.

The Contributions of Ham's Descendants. The Hamites built the pyramids, invented paper, ceramics, architecture, and sailboats. Hamites domesticated animals, governed running waters, were the first to make pulleys, to smelt iron, to create clocks or calendars, to chart maps and to make gears. All of this came from the descendants of Ham. Ham and his descendants have rendered an extraordinary service to humankind.[7]

All of the earlier civilizations of note were found and carried to their highest technical proficiency by Hamitic people. There is scarcely a basic technological invention which cannot be traced to the descendants of Ham.

Most of us have been taught that Indo-Europeans are the most inventive people in the world. This is a culturally-conditioned prejudice. To rid oneself of it requires a fresh, objective examination of the origins of technological achievement. One can trace almost any element of our highly complex civilization—be it aircraft, paper weaving, propulsion systems, explosives, medical technology, mechanical principles, or the use of electricity—to Hamitic people. It is not possible to trace these inventions to the descendants of Japheth or Shem. Technology originally contributed by descendants of Shem or Japheth can be counted on one hand. This can be supported by over 1,000 pieces of archaeological and other evidence.[8]

African inventors' technological superiority continued from ancient history to African American inventors. African Americans invented telephone systems, fountain pens, traffic lights, ironing boards, railway switches, bicycle frames, refrigerators, baby carriages, clothes dryers, typewriters, lawn mowers, guitars, printing presses, batteries, hand stamps, and elevators. African Americans are Black Hamitic people.[9]

Egyptians (descendants of Mizraim) were fiction writers and poets. They also practiced medicine. In fact, they compiled the first catalogue of medicine, called the *Material Medica.* Forget about Hippocrates being the father of medicine. Black people were the fathers of medicine. They perfected many sciences such as the science of embalming.[10]

We still can't figure out the mysteries of the pyramids. The descendants of Mizraim perfected them too. They laid elaborate systems of water irrigation. They also gave us cloister lighting which is still used in many cathedrals today.

The Cushites also developed the formula for calculating the rectangle. By 2,000 B.C. they had developed uniform multiplication tables and square roots. By the year 2,000 B.C. they had invented writing and signature seals to sign their letters. They also developed the first grammar system including pronouns. The Cushite city of Aick was called Cush Town and was famous for its library. It contained the sacred writings that were buried there before the Flood.[11]

Cushites had libraries of over 30,000 volumes of books. They compiled the first grammar and bilingual dictionaries, with 50,000 tables. The Cushite libraries had 20,000 volumes that were mounted on cylinders and revolving stands. They made dictionaries, encyclopedias, and works of law, science and literature. Isn't it strange that white people told Black people that all Africans know how to do is run around in grass skirts.[12]

There is evidence that Cushites in Nubia made the pyramids first and brought the technology to Egypt. Markings on walls show that Cushites were superior in art, had a luxurious civilization and were people of great knowledge. They invented the chisel, the saw, the hammer, and the wheel. They were the masters of architecture, including towers and temples. The later Cushite empires of Songhai, Mali and Ghana were renowned for their government systems, libraries, and wealth. Other creations of the Cushites included the Universities of Timbuktu, Sankhore and Janay. There were 1400 faculty members at the University of Janay. Students came from distant nations to study medicine, history, astronomy and higher mathematics. They even came there to study the sacred text. Doctors there taught men how to perform limb transplants and other medical techniques such as cataract surgery.[13]

Black Nations in Scripture. Of the 70 nations mentioned in the Bible, 14 come from Japheth, 26 come from Shem, and 30 come from Ham. Hamitic nations are mentioned more frequently than European nations. From Genesis to Revelation, Blacks are ethnically present.[14]

Rome is mentioned 20 times in the New Testament and not at all in the Old Testament. Greece is mentioned 26 times in the New Testament and four times in the Old Testament. Hamitic cities are mentioned much more frequently. For example, Sidon is mentioned 17 times. Tyre is mentioned 57 times. Cush is mentioned 40 times. Canaanites are mentioned 153 times, and Egypt is mentioned 727 times.[15]

This totals over 1,000 biblical mentions of Hamitic nations. One could wonder why we are looking for the African presence in the Bible. Perhaps we need to find out where the white folks are!

Black Personalities in Scripture. Biblical evidence exists that Adam and Eve were Black. The first nation mentioned in the Bible was Africa, and many scholars believe that the Garden of Eden was located either in or near Africa (Genesis 2:8). In fact, recently a group of renowned anthropologists concluded that Adam and Eve were Africans. A Black Adam and Eve appeared on the front cover of *Newsweek*, January 11, 1988.[16] The article provided scientific evidence that Black people are present and accounted for in Scripture.

Nimrod, another biblical figure is often portrayed badly by whites (Genesis 10:8). The fact of the matter is he was a powerful Black brother. The Bible calls him a mighty one. The Hebrew word for mighty one is *gabor*. It means giant chieftain, super hero, champion. The brother was so tough that he fought wild animals with his bare hands! He was the world's first empire builder. He founded Babylon. It was Nimrod who founded great nations.[17]

The wife of Joseph, Asenath was an Hamitic woman (Genesis 41:45). If Joseph was the patriarch of Manesseh, then these two Israelite tribes had Black blood flowing through their veins.[18]

39

The Queen of Sheba, mentioned in 1 Kings 10, was a beautiful Black woman. Her name was Makeda. She was a great administrator and an international stateswoman. She ruled part of Egypt, Ethiopia, Arabia and Syria, with justice, fortitude and wisdom for 50 years. Solomon was in love with this Black woman. He called her the fairest of the fairest (Song of Solomon 1:5).[19] The Miss America and Miss USA pageants are just finding out what Solomon always knew.

Ebedmelech in Jeremiah 38:7-9 was a Black man. Unfortunately, the King James translators tried to castrate our Ethiopian brother. They called him a eunuch, but the proper translation of the Hebrew word from which they derived "eunuch" is really "official." The brother was a high official in the Jerusalem court, and he was the one who rescued Jeremiah from the pit.[20]

Two famous kings of the Bible were Black. One is Tirhakah in 2 Kings 19. There we find Hezekiah needing help because Sennacherib was coming after him. God told him, "Don't worry about Sennacherib because there is a brother, a Black brother, the Mike Tyson of kings." The brother is so bad that all God had to do was mention his name. Another famous Black king was Shishak (1 Kings 14:25), the great African pharaoh who was so mighty that the Jewish kings gave up and surrendered to him without a fight.[21]

In 2 Chronicles 14:9 we notice that Jethro was African. He was a Midianite. The old term for Midianite was *Chem*. This was a form of Cush, meaning Black. This Black brother was the one who instructed Moses on how to organize the Children of Israel.

David's great–grandmother was Rahab, a Canaanite woman (Joshua 2:1). That means David had Black blood flowing through his veins. Solomon's mother was Bathsheba (2 Samuel 11). The name "Bathsheba" means daughter of Sheba, a tribe of Cush. Scripture doesn't provide the information to show that Moses was racially Black, but everything else about him was. He was born in Africa (Exodus 2:1),

40

trained in Africa (Exodus 3:1-11), and his name was African. Everything about the brother was African.

There were many Blacks in the New Testament. Simon of Cyrene, the man who helped Jesus carry His cross, the last person to help our Saviour before He died, was Black (Mark 15:21).[22]

Rufus, the son of Simon was Black (Mark 15). Lucius and Simeon were Black brothers who ordained Paul (Acts 13:1-8). Paul's ministry began with Black folks. The Apostle Paul himself was a Benjamite. Benjamites came from Kish, and the word *Kish* is one of the forms of Cush. Then there is the Ethiopian Eunuch (Acts 8:26-40). Many say he was responsible for the Ethiopian Catholic church.

It is evident that from Genesis to Revelation, from creation to redemption, from Alpha to Omega, from the first Adam to the last Adam, from B.C. to A.D., Blacks are there, numerically and biographically. In Isaiah 18 God says that Black people were awesome from the beginning.

Why Knowledge of the Black Presence in Scripture Is Important. Truth affects self–esteem. Truth causes the walls of Jericho to fall down. Truth instills hope. With truth, God is sending a revival to a Black community. His truth is marching on. The truth no longer needs to be suppressed. The truth is marching on. The truth is an idea whose time has come. It is an irresistible force that has no immovable object.

Truth is a light that no darkness can comprehend. Truth is larger than denominations. It is larger than any ecclesiastical body. It is larger than any religious judiciary. It is larger than church tribunals. It is larger than any sectarian group. Truth is larger than conventions, convocations and conferences. It is larger than Jaguars, Porches and Rolls Royces. It is larger than deacons, ushers that don't usher, or trustees that don't trust.

Truth is bigger than narrow-minded Black leaders, blinded Jewish leaders, or bigoted white leaders. This is the hour of Truth! God has brought Black people to the kingdom for such a time as this. The train of truth is rolling and nothing can stop it because the Holy Ghost is behind it!

BIBLE STUDY APPLICATION

Instructions: The following exercises provide the opportunity to study some Canaanites who were, in one way or another, in the life of Christ. The first five exercises consist of discovery questions, followed by summary questions. The sixth exercise provides the opportunity to apply information from this chapter to a church-based ministry. The seventh exercise is for personal application.

"These are the three sons of Noah: and of them was the whole earth overspread. Now these are the generations of the sons of Noah, Shem, Ham, and Japheth: and unto them were sons born after the flood. And the sons of Ham; Cush, and Mizraim, and Phut, and Canaan. And the sons of Cush; Sheba, and Havilah, and Sabtah, and Raahmah, and Sabtecha: and the sons of Raahmah; Sheba, and Dedan. And Cush begat Nimrod: he began to be a mighty one in the earth. And Mizraim begat Ludim, and Anamim, and Lehabim, and Naphtuhim, And Pathrusim, and Casluhim, (out of whom came Philistim,) and Caphtorim.

And Canaan begat Sidon his firstborn, and Heth, And the Jebusite, and the Amorite, and the Girgasite, And the Hivite, and the Arkite, and the Sinite, And the Arvadite, and the Zemarite, and the Hamathite: and afterward were the families of the Canaanites spread abroad. And the border of the Canaanites was from Sidon, as thou comest to Gerar, unto Gaza; as thou goest, unto Sodom, and Gomorrah, and Admah, and Zeboim, even unto Lasha. These are the sons of Ham, after their families, after their tongues, in their countries, and in their nations" (Genesis 9:19; 10:1, 6-20).

1. The Canaanites - no. 1

The father of Canaan was Ham, the father of Black nations. The word Ham, in Hebrew, means dark, or "burnt–faced."

a. Who were the immediate relatives of Canaan? (Genesis 10:6)

b. How many nations did the descendants of Canaan found? (Genesis 10:15-20)

c. Over how much territory did the Canaanites spread? (Genesis 10:18-20; Numbers 34:3-12)

d. How did the descendants of Shem (Jews) make contact with the descendants of Canaan? (Genesis 12:5-6; 38:1-4; Deuteronomy 7:1; Joshua 10:1; 11:1-5; 15:63)

e. What evidence is there that intermarriage took place between the descendants of Canaan and the descendants of Shem? (Genesis 12:5-6; 34:2, 9, 16; Deuteronomy 7:1; Joshua 9:7-16; 15:63)

f. SUMMARY QUESTION: In what sense are the Canaanites a part of African American history? Explain.

2. Rahab

Rahab is a Canaanite woman who was a part of the genealogy of Christ.

a. Where did Rahab live? (Joshua 2:1)

b. In what sense was Jericho a part of Canaan? (Deuteronomy 34:1-14; Joshua 2:1-2)

c. What did Rahab do for the spies whom Joshua sent to explore the land of Canaan? (Joshua 2:1-23)

d. In your opinion, why should Rahab be included in the Hebrews "Faith Hall of Fame"? (Hebrews 11:30)

e. What relation was Rahab to Jesus Christ? (Matthew 1:1-17)

f. SUMMARY QUESTION: Of what significance is it to the self-esteem of African American women that one of Jesus' great-grandmothers was Black?

3. Tamar

Tamar is a witness that the Lord can turn a bad situation around for good.

a. What evidence is there that Tamar was a Canaanite? (Genesis 38:1-6)

b. Could Tamar have children? (Genesis 38:6-11)

c. What evidence is there that Tamar's problems had "gotten to her"? (Genesis 38:12-19)

d. What eventually happened to Tamar? (Genesis 38:20-30)

e. What relationship was Tamar to Jesus Christ? (Matthew 1:1-17)

f. SUMMARY QUESTION: Of what significance is the story of Tamar for women in general? Of what significance is it for African American women? How does it dispel the myth that the Bible is a "white man's book, written by, for and about white people?"

4. Ruth

Ruth became one of the great-grandmothers of our Lord Jesus Christ.

a. From what country was Ruth? (Ruth 1:1-4) Who was the founder of the country from which Ruth came? (Genesis 19:30-37)

b. Who was the father of the founder of the country from

which Ruth came? (Genesis 11:27-28) Who was the uncle of the founder of the country from which Ruth came? (11:27) Who was the grandfather of the uncle of the founder of Ruth's native country? (11:27) In what town did this grandfather grow up? (11:28)

c. Who founded the kingdom of Babylon (home of Ur the Chaldees)? (Genesis 10:6)

d. What are some highlights of Ruth's life? (Ruth 1:1-19; 2:1-2; 3:1-3; 4:13-22)

e. What relationship was Ruth to our Lord Jesus Christ? (Matthew 1:1-6)

f. SUMMARY QUESTION: In Hebrew, the name Ham means "dark" or "burnt–faced." What indication is there that Ruth was a Black woman? Of what significance is this to the self–esteem of African American women? Is the Bible merely a white man's Bible written for, by and about white people?

5. Bathsheba

Bathsheba, the woman with whom David had an adulterous affair, was a Black woman who is named in the genealogy of Christ.

a. Who was Bathsheba's husband? (2 Samuel 11:3) From what nation was he? (2 Samuel 23:39) Who was the founder of the Hittites? (Genesis 23:3, 5, 7, 10, 16, 18, 20; 25:10; 49:32)

b. Who was Heth's father? (Genesis 10:5) Who was Heth's grandfather? (Genesis 10:6)

c. Who was Bathsheba's father? (2 Samuel 11:3) Who was Bathsheba's grandfather? (2 Samuel 23:34) Where was her grandfather from? (2 Samuel 15:12)

d. Where was Bathsheba's grandfather's hometown located? (Joshua 15:20, 50) Which tribe of Israel took over this land which was already occupied by Canaanites? (Joshua 15:20)

45

Who was the father of Canaan? (Genesis 10:6)

e. What are the highlights from Bathsheba's life? (2 Samuel 11:1–4, 14–27)

f. SUMMARY QUESTION: What are the indications that Bathsheba was probably a Black woman? What indications are there, in her story, that the Lord can take a bad situation and turn it around for good?

6. CHURCH–BASED MINISTRY

Suppose that you were given the assignment to plan a men's or women's Bible study that would focus on the presence of Black women or men in the Bible. Create a list of topics for the class. How would the class be organized? Could the contents be used for an evangelistic Bible study? If so, how?

7. PERSONAL APPLICATION

Of what personal significance is it to you that there are at least four Black women who were great–grandmothers of our Lord Jesus Christ? How does it affect the images that surface in your mind as you read Scripture?

CHAPTER TWO

"President Vetoes Unemployment Compensation Bill!" Stephanie caught a glimpse of this headline while watching the school bus drive away with her three children. The article said that the president vetoed a bill to extend the number of weeks that families could receive unemployment benefits. Panic set in as she recalled, just days ago, receiving the pink slip that terminated her job.

Stephanie had worked as a typist with a parts factory for more than twenty years. She couldn't imagine what she would do now that the factory was moving to India. Nearly everyone in the neighborhood who worked there was being terminated. She thought about how she had just reached her 43rd birthday. "Who will hire me now? That is the only place I have ever worked," she thought, as she put on her coat and started toward the unemployment compensation office.

In December 1990, the Bureau of Labor Statistics reported that the rate of unemployment for African Americans was more than twice that of the white population.[1] By the end of 1990, the rate for Blacks hovered around 13% compared to a 6.9% rate for whites.[2] Moreover, the U.S. Department of Commerce reported that, at the opening of the decade, 43.2% of African American families with children under 18 years of age were living in poverty, compared to 14.1% for white families.[3] Rates of homelessness continue to soar, even though there are no accurate statistics to reflect the true extent of the problem.

The Department of Commerce reports that 25.9% of Black families have incomes that are less than $10,000 per year, compared to only 7.7% for whites.[4] The most recent census reports the average African American family having a net worth (ownership of property, insurance, valuables, etc.) of $4,170, compared $43,280 for the average white family.[5] This situation is in part caused by plants continuing to close, businesses continuing to move overseas, and national and local governments continuing to remove legislation which traditionally protected families from poverty.

These dramatic plunges into poverty have become most visible in the plight of the homeless, so common in many of the communities that surround African American churches. Yet, according to research by Eric Lincoln and Lawrence Mamiya, most African American churches have not created ministries which deal with this issue.

In "The Black Church in the African American Experience," Eric Lincoln and Lawrence Mamiya present interviews of 2,150 church representatives concerning their outreach programs. They reported that only 114 (5.3%) church representatives said they were cooperating with employment agencies to solve unemployment problems in their communities. Only 157 (7.3%) interacted with welfare rights groups and only 146 (6.8%) had food or clothing programs of any type (Lincoln, 1990).

All of these statistics paint a picture of thousands of people such as Stephanie, in the opening case study, being plunged into poverty with nowhere to turn. However, that is only part of the story. In the following excerpt Dr. Jeremiah A. Wright, Jr., pastor of Trinity United Church of Christ, reminds us that there is hope. He says that Jesus can take the "little bit" and go a "long way" with it.

IN NEED OF A MIRACLE

Dr. Jeremiah A. Wright, Jr.
1 Kings 17:8-16

The woman in 1 Kings 17 sounds like many women who have sat in my office, and like women who sit in our midst week after week. This is a single parent who is trying to raise a child, with the double burden of trying to raise a man child all by herself. She is a mama much like many of our mamas, with no money, no man, and a "no win" situation. There is no way to feed herself, and no way to feed her son. She is just doing like my grandmother used to call "making do."

It has always been amazing to me how country folk could take next to nothing and "make do." My daddy did the cooking in our home, and Daddy could take nothing and make a feast, and it would make you filled up. It would make you feel like you had just been to a banquet. Sometimes he had just about the same ingredients as this woman in 1 Kings, out in the country near Sidon. All she had was a handful of flour, and a little oil.

She reminds me of Daddy who would take a little bit of flour and put it in the white lima beans, or in those great northern or navy beans to make the consistency thicker. He could make it so that it would stick to your bones, and make you feel like you'd eaten much more than you actually had. A handful of flour would "make do."

Daddy would take leftover mashed potatoes and sometimes leftover boiled potatoes and mash them up. He would take a handful of flour, some seasoning and sometimes a little onion and make some potato cakes, put them in a frying pan and, with just a little bit of oil, make you think that you had eaten a seven course meal. He could take a handful of flour and make do.

Daddy would take flour and make biscuits, not frozen biscuits from the supermarket. He would make biscuits from scratch. On

49

the "high-falutin'" days, we'd put butter on the biscuits and pour some syrup (either Alaga, or Karo or Grandma's black strap molasses). We knew we were living "high on the hog" when we got Log Cabin or that fast-moving stuff, because we had used a syrup that was much slower than Heinz coming out of a bottle. It was syrup and biscuits—a meal fit for a king!

Then on the "get down days" (meaning when we couldn't afford syrup), Daddy would take a handful of flour and a little oil and make gravy for the biscuits. He'd put the flour in after the oil had gotten hot, and stir it until it got thick and brown. He would season the biscuits while he was stirring them. Then "by and by" he would add water and keep on stirring, so it wouldn't have lumps. Nothing was worse than lumpy gravy. I remember that gravy running all down on those biscuits, and all over the plate. It was made from just a little bit of flour—a handful of flour—and a little bit of oil. This was "making do."

Daddy could take flour and make dumplings. Some of you don't know anything about dumplings. Perhaps you have never seen a dumpling. I used to think dumplings were part of the chicken. I think I was in college, in a biology class, dissecting a chicken, before I discovered that there was no part of a chicken called dumplings. Most of our children have never seen a chicken foot. My Daddy could take chicken feet, chicken necks, chicken giblets, flour, and those big old dumplings and make you feel like you had eaten a whole turkey on Thanksgiving Day. A handful of nothing would "make do."

Daddy learned how to cook down in the country, in a town where they would use a little piece of fatback to season the cabbage. It wasn't enough to feed anyone. It was just enough to make the cabbage slippery, and make the house smell good. It was enough to make a person feel like s/he was in heaven. The Black mamas down in the country taught us how to make do. They would take next to nothing and build giants in every field.

Well, this woman in 1 Kings 17:12 was doing just that. She was making do with a handful of flour and a little bit of olive oil in a jar. The Bible says she went to get what my people used to call "kindling wood" to make a fire so that she could heat some hot water and make stove-top bread or make some gravy with that oil.

Times were hard for this single parent. Not only was she broke, but she was also living in a recession. The Bible says the brook dried up and the food ran out. She didn't know where her next meal was coming from, or how she would provide for her child. Have you ever had someone depending on you, looking to you for help, looking to you for substance, looking to you for something to eat and you didn't have the help to give? Isn't it an awful feeling? Talking about helpless and hopeless, have you ever heard a baby cry itself to sleep hungry? It's a different type of sound. It is an awful sound. It is a sound that can haunt you all of the way over into the daytime.

When a baby cries, most of us get up and give it a bottle or a breast and put it back to sleep. But it is a different story when there is no milk either in the bottle or in the breast, when there is no water, no food, no lights, no heat, no surplus, no mate, and nowhere to turn. However, there is the screech of a little one looking up at you with trusting eyes, wondering why you won't do something about the pain in his belly. Those screeches will give you nightmares in the daytime.

The woman in 1 Kings 17 was down to her last meal. She was broken, burdened, defeated, depressed, and wondering what in the world she should do next. Have you ever done all that you can do and that still isn't good enough? Have you ever done all you can do and wondered what to do next? This woman in 1 Kings 17 was in that state. She was a woman in need of a miracle. She was where some of us are right now. She was in need of a miracle.

At the moment that I am writing, I know of three different people in three different health crises who are in need of a miracle. One member lies in a coma. The EEG says that there is no hope. That member is in need of a miracle. Another member

51

has a blood disorder and the doctors can't determine what it is or what to do with it. He doesn't know whether it is leukemia, sickle cell anemia, mononucleosis, a plasma deficiency, or a hemoflagellate. The doctors don't know. The specialists don't know. The hematologists don't know. This person is in need of a miracle.

Yet another person faces a surgeon's scalpel with the possibility that the tissue to be removed is cancerous. She just finished her chemotherapy, and surgery is coming soon. Another person just started her chemotherapy but there is no surgery that can help her. These people are in need of a miracle.

Then there are unemployed people. Some may try to be "cool" because they don't want anyone to know. There are people who thought they would be out of work for only a little while, perhaps a couple of weeks, or a month at the most. However, now they are feeling like this woman in 1 Kings 17:12. Things are beginning to look desperate. The month has turned into six months, then eight months and then more than a year. These are people in need of a miracle.

When families are thrown into a crisis, tempers often flare, words fly, objects get thrown and fists get used, before someone makes an appointment with a counselor or a lawyer. When this happens, people realize that they are in need of a miracle! Then there are stubborn people who say they don't need help, but their marriage is on the way to hell in a handbasket. They are in need of a miracle.

In a crisis, a Black man may hit his wife. Why does a brother as strong as this hit the crown of God's creation even though she is as soft as she is? Judge Pincham says it's because he can't be what he hasn't seen. He hasn't seen a Black man who is tough in the world, but tender with his woman. He hasn't see someone who is tough in the board room and tender in the bedroom. He hasn't seen someone who is tough with his fellows but tender with his family. If he hasn't seen it, he can't be it. He can't be what he can't see. This is someone who is in the process of destroying that which means the most to him, in the entire world. He doesn't know why, but he can't stop what he is doing. He wants to stop but he can't. He has a case of what my mommy used to call, "the can't help its." This brother whose options are limited because his perspective is limited, is in need of a miracle!

Like the woman in our text, the readers of this chapter may be at the end of their resources. There is no relief in sight. There is no change in the situation. There is no dramatic turnaround in the way things are going. You have prayed and prayed, until you feel that you just have prayed out. You are in need of a miracle!

You may be "down" on yourself. You may have a habit and the habit is controlling you. You have tried 29 days in–patient programs and you have slipped and fallen again. You have tried AA and NA and Free 'n' One. You have even tried talking to yourself, but nothing works! Today you are right back where you were the first day that you woke up in the pigpen and came to yourself. You have tried and you have tried, but you keep on "messing up." You are in need of a miracle.

Perhaps your finances are in shambles. You look good every Sunday morning, but you haven't got a quarter in savings, and you are up to your "kazoo" in debt. Those credit cards and that other plastic has gotten you so behind the eight ball that you can't even begin to hope to see daylight. You owe everybody and you are late on everything!

Tithing sounds like a curse word to you because you haven't got enough now to make it from payday to payday. (Just a little secret footnote here; you don't tithe with what you have left. You give God God's part first and watch what a difference that makes. End of footnote.) However, you don't feel that you can do that now, because you are one step away from Chapter 13. You are in need of a miracle!

You may be smiling on the outside, but hurting on the inside. The pain does not go away. You don't see anyone who really understands. No one listens without coming out of a phony "holy bag" on you, and saying, "Oh honey, you just pray about it." You have given up on trying to find authentic friendship. Everything you do is at a superficial level, but deep down you are dying. You are slowly dying. You need to talk to someone, but no one seems to care about you genuinely as a person.

Have you any idea what it is like to try to tell someone what is inside of you, deep down in your gut, and have them cut you off, or try to "hit on" you? Do you know what that's like? Do you know what it is like to be grappling with life and death issues with someone and they start talking about something they saw on a talk show or a soap? Have you ever been talking about your life with someone and they started flirting with you? Have you ever started talking about children dying for no reason and the other person started talking about some pop theology, and never heard what it is you are saying? Then you give up, you smile and praise God, but you hurt and ask God why! You are in need of a miracle!

Like this woman in 1 Kings 17, you have done all that you can do, and you can't do any more. Well, if you need a miracle and you are in the Lord's will number one, you are in good company. Look at the company you keep! First there is Abraham, up on the mountain. He has a knife in his hand. He has a knot in his throat. His son is on the altar and there are questions on his mind. Abraham was in need of a miracle! Look at the company you keep!

Then there is Moses down at the Red Sea with an angry ocean in front of him. Pharaoh's army is in back of him! Impossible mountains are on each side of him, and an impossible situation is surrounding him. Moses was in need of a miracle! Look at the company you keep!

Then there is Joshua. Joshua is standing outside of the walls of Jericho with nothing but a ram's horn in his hand. Joshua was in need of a miracle! Look at the company you keep!

Then there was Hannah, she had no child, a barren womb, a woman mocking her and making fun of her. Hannah was in need of a miracle! Look at the company you keep! Then there was Deborah and Gideon on Mount Tabor facing Sisera's entire army. Deborah was in need of a miracle! Look at the company you keep! Then there was Ruth, she had no man, no money, no way of making it, and no way of getting back home! Ruth was in need of a miracle! Look at the company you keep!

Then there was David. He was looking at a giant with only a sling shot and five smooth stones. There was Mandela in prison for 27 years for something he did not do! There was Queen Nzinga, facing the entire Portuguese army with nothing but a few loyal troops, and a whole lot of faith! There was Rosa Parks facing the Birmingham police with nothing but some tired feet and a "made up mind." If you need a miracle today, look at the company you keep!

That is the first point. The second point is that, not only are you in good company, but you're also in good hands. You can face whatever it is that you are facing that seems impossible! I've got some news for you! You are in good hands! First of all, God knows what you need! Don't get so focused on the problem that you forget the one who provides for problems.

Let's look at 1 Kings 17 again, at verse 7. When the brook dried up, it was like a recession. The brook dried up, the job ran out, the money dried up, and patience ran out. Problems got worse. The stage was set for an awful ending. Then in verse 12, we hear the cry of despair and the handwriting on the wall.

You may be like this woman. All you have is a handful of flour and a little bit of oil. All you have is a life of broken dreams and broken promises. All you have is a body that used to be healthy but now it is all used up. All you have is a boy to raise and a daddy who is not around. You have gotten tired of making grown folks do what they ought to do naturally. All you have is a loveless marriage. All you have are bills to pay and no way to pay them. All you have is the habit you can't break and the relationship you can't take.

All this woman had was a handful of flour and what little she had was barely enough for her son and her. She knew it would be her last meal. Then they might starve to death.

However, if we look at verse 7 and then skip to verse 12 we miss verse 8. In verse 8 we see God has got this woman's address! God knows exactly where she lives! God knows precisely what she's got and what she's going through! God knows just what she needs! God knows your address too. He knows your phone number! He knows your private number! God knows exactly where you live, precisely what you're going through and just what it is you need. You're in good hands because God knows what you need.

Secondly you are in good hands because God has already made a way. What the woman in 1 Kings 17 didn't know was that God had already made a way. What you and I need to remember when we're in need of a miracle is that God has already made a way. We may not see it right now. We might be looking right at it and not see it because sometimes God sends a miracle in something ordinary, like in a bowl or a jar. We may miss God's miracle because we are looking for the extraordinary! You may not be able to see it, but look again! God is already making a way! You are in good hands.

You are in good hands not only because God knows what you need, not only because God has already made a way but because God is still working, even when you can't see how He is working! Read what the woman in 1 Kings 17 did. She kept going back to that bowl and looking at it, again and again. Then she looked around to see if anyone else was looking! She could not see or understand how God was doing what God was doing! But Thank God for the way God works!

He works completely independently of what we can see, or understand, or figure out. He is independent of our ability or inability to piece our lives together. God works in mysterious ways! His wonders to perform! He plants His feet upon the waves and rides on every storm! We may not be able to see how, but that is how the Lord works. He is still working even when we can't see Him. He is still working even when we can't understand. That is how the Lord works.

He may not come when you want Him. Right now Black folks want an answer to problems. Black folks want the Lord to come now, but He may not come when we want Him.

Family members are sick and dying. They are sick in the mind, sick in body and sick in spirit. We want the Lord to come right now, but He may not come when we want Him. Single parents want help now. They want the Lord to come now, but He may not come when we want Him.

Your marriage may be in a mess and pain is in your hearts. Stubbornness hurts, and you want some help right now, but He may not come when you want Him. When you've got more months left than you've got money left you want the Lord right now. But He may not come when you want Him.

Oh, but He's fixing it. That's now the Lord works. That's just like God. He may not come when you want Him but He will come on time!!

BIBLE STUDY APPLICATION

Instructions: This Bible study provides the opportunity to examine the story of the widow (found in 1 Kings 17) more closely. The first five exercises consist of five "discovery" questions and a summary question. The sixth exercise provides the opportunity to apply principles from this chapter to a church-based ministry. The seventh exercise encourages you to make a personal application of the contents of this chapter.

"And the word of the LORD came unto him, saying, Arise, get thee to Zarephath, which belongeth to Zidon, and dwell there: behold, I have commanded a widow woman there to sustain thee. So he arose and went to Zarephath. And when he came to the gate of the city, behold, the widow woman was there gathering

of sticks: and he called to her, and said, Fetch me, I pray thee, a little water in a vessel, that I may drink. And as she was going to fetch it, he called to her, and said, Bring me, I pray thee, a morsel of bread in thine hand.

And she said, As the Lord thy God liveth, I have not a cake, but an handful of meal in a barrel, and a little oil in a cruse: and, behold, I am gathering two sticks, that I may go in and dress it for me and my son, that we may eat it, and die. And Elijah said unto her, Fear not; go and do as thou hast said: but make me thereof a little cake first, and bring it unto me, and after make for thee and for thy son. For thus saith the Lord God of Israel, The barrel of meal shall not waste, neither shall the cruse of oil fail, until the day that the Lord sendeth rain upon the earth. And she went and did according to the saying of Elijah: and she, and he, and her house, did eat many days. And the barrel of meal wasted not, neither did the cruse of oil fail, according to the word of the Lord, which he spake by Elijah" (1 Kings 17:8-16).

1. God's Concern for Widows

There is evidence that the widow believed in the one true God (1 Kings 7:12, 24). God provided for widows in the Mosaic Law. However, by all indications, the Jews of the Northern Kingdom were not practicing these laws.

a. What is one way God provided for widows? (Deuteronomy 14:27-29; 26:12-15)

b. What is another way that God provided for widows? (Deuteronomy 14:27-29; 26:12-15)

c. What special protections were there for widows? (Psalm

94:6; Ezekiel 22:7; Malachi 3:5)

d. What is yet another way that God provided for widows? (Deuteronomy 24:19-22)

e. What indication is there that Israel under Ahab (king of the Northern Kingdom) may not have been following the Mosaic Law? (1 Kings 16:29-33)

f. SUMMARY QUESTION: Today, thousands of African American mothers are homeless and without regular meals for their children, and the national, state and local governments are not dealing with this crisis. What do these homeless women have in common with the widow of Mark 9?

2. Was the Widow of 1 Kings 17 Black?

The widow of 1 Kings 17 may have been a Black woman.

a. Zarephath was near Sidon. According to the Bible, who was the father of Sidon, for whom the town was named? (1 Kings 17:9; Genesis 10:6, 15)

b. The word Ham means "hot" or "heat" in Hebrew. Who was the father of Canaan, Sidon's father, and what lands did the descendants of Canaan's father populate? (Genesis 10:6-20)

c. What specific lands did Sidon populate? (Genesis 10:15-19)

d. Sidon was one of several Phoenician city-states. Of what importance was it, at one time, in the history of the Jews? (Joshua 13:6; Judges 3:3; 18:7; 1 Kings 16:31; 17:9; Isaiah 23:11-12; Jeremiah 27:3; Zechariah 9:2; Joel 3:1-5)

e. Who were some famous biblical Sidonians or Phoenicians? (1 Kings 16:31; Mark 7:24-31; Mark 3:8; Luke 6:17; Acts 12:20; 27:3)

f. SUMMARY QUESTION: While the widow was from a very important group of people with a glorious past, her current precarious situation did not allow her to feel like a person of such an important group. In this respect, how is this woman similar to many African Americans today?

3. The Climate of the Times

The widow lived in the Northern Kingdom of Israel during the reign of the evil King Ahab. It was a time of political and economic chaos.

a. Describe the drought that was spreading across the land. (1 Kings 17:1; 18:1-6)

b. Describe the political climate. (2 Chronicles 13:1-3, 17-19; 1 Kings 15:1-9, 23-33; 16:8-30)

c. How many changes of government had occurred over a period of 72 years? (2 Chronicles 13:1-3, 17-19; 1 Kings 15:1-9, 23-33; 16:8-30)

d. What is one circumstance that could have plunged this woman into widowhood? (1 Kings 15:25-29; 16:8-12, 15-19; 17:1)

e. What environment was created by the worshipers of Baal and Ashtoreth? (1 Kings 14:23, 24; 15:12-13; 21:1, 7; 2 Kings 23:7; Deuteronomy 23:15-18)

f. SUMMARY QUESTION: What indications are there that the poor widow might not be able to depend on the government for help? Draw parallels between this widow woman and Black women raising children alone today.

4. The Role of Elijah the Prophet

At the moment that so many Black women have reached the end of their resources, the Lord has sent a powerful man or woman of God to help them.

a. In what type of political situation did Elijah live? (1 Kings 16:29-34)

b. Why did Elijah have to hide first at Cherith Brook and then in a town called Zarephath? (1 Kings 17:1-9)

c. How did Elijah and the widow woman at Zarephath help one another? (1 Kings 17:8-24)

d. Why did Elijah have to flee to Beersheba? (1 Kings 18:16—19:3)

e. Eventually, what happened to Elijah? (2 Kings 2:1-12)

f. SUMMARY QUESTION: What are some similarities between Elijah and African American pastors of today? Why
is the role of the "undershepherd" important in the life of
the Black community?

5. God Comes on Time

The widow was all by herself. She was facing two major
crises. It seems that God came to her aid right on time.

a. What was one crisis that the widow faced? (1 Kings 17:12)

b. What was another crisis that the widow faced? (1 Kings
17:17)

c. How did the Lord work through Elijah in the first crisis? (1
Kings 17:13-16)

d. How did the Lord work through Elijah in the second crisis?
(1 Kings 17:19-24)

e. Specifically how did the widow help Elijah? (1 Kings 17:15)

f. SUMMARY QUESTION: There are many parallels between the relationship between Elijah and the widow and
the relationship between the African American church and
troubled Black people today. What are some of them?

6. CHURCH–BASED MINISTRY

Are there some practical ways in which your church could
come to the assistance of the unemployed, the homeless, or
people in poverty? Describe (or create an improvement in) at
least one ministry or auxiliary that could meet this need.

7. PERSONAL APPLICATION

Are you at the end of your resources in some area of your life?
If so, review this chapter and seek the Lord for an answer.

61

CHAPTER THREE

Jacky was sitting at the kitchen, watching the TV show "Soap" when Danny, her husband came in from work. Before he could take off his coat, Jacky began telling him the news of the day. She had found some marijuana in their son Michael's biology book.

"I had just finished taking my morning aspirins when I noticed Michael's book on the table. It seemed kind of interesting, so I was just looking at it. Then I came across this little plastic bag of marijuana stuffed between the pages," she said.

"Did you ask him about it?" Danny said, sitting down at the table.

"Yeah, and he made like he didn't know what it was. He said that some of the kids at school probably put it there," answered Jacky, pouring her third cup of coffee.

By then, Danny was pouring a can of beer, along with some whiskey for a "kicker," and his hand was moving over toward the television to change the channel to Monday night football.

Jacky got up to take sleeping pills that she had gotten at the store, while Danny started on his second can of beer.

"Don't worry about it, Jacky," Danny finally said. "You're a worry wort.

"But I can't help it," Jacky said, gulping down the

sleeping pills, and braiding her hair. "Haven't you seen the way he's been acting lately? Haven't you noticed how red and glassy his eyes are?"

"He's a big boy, Jacky. Leave him alone. I know what's wrong with you, baby," Danny laughed, turning up the volume on the television. "You're a crisis addict! That's a term I heard over one of those talk shows. A crisis addict! You're hung up on worrying," he said, pouring himself another "kicker."

When the term addiction is used, most people probably think of illegal drugs. However, addictions come in many varieties, and they don't always involve the use of illegal drugs. In the opening case study, at least seven possible addictions are mentioned. In fact, there are so many types of addictions in American society, that some psychologists are now using the term, "addictive personality" to describe certain predispositions toward addiction.

One of the outcomes of an addictive personality that has not come under the Lordship of Jesus Christ, is addiction to dangerous substances, usually classified as illegal drugs. Of course, teenagers represent one of the groups in American society that is most seriously affected by the current widespread use of illegal drugs. In a recent Gallup Poll, teenagers across the United States were asked to state what they feel is the biggest problem facing people their age. Fifty-four percent of all teenagers felt that drug abuse was the biggest problem. The percentage for African American teenagers was 55%.[1]

In the following sermon, Dr. James Forbes discusses the problem of addiction among Christians and non-Christians, and presents a spiritual approach to dealing with the problem.

A WORD ABOUT ADDICTIONS

Dr. James Forbes
Mark 9:14-29

In Mark the ninth chapter, we see that when they brought Jesus to this man, the man said to Him, "Listen, Your disciples couldn't do it, but sir, can You do anything?" Jesus stopped him. "Don't say 'if.' If you can believe all things are possible. I'm able to fill this person's space. I am able to set him free from enslavement. Don't say if! All things are possible!"

When they brought the boy to Jesus, instead of the boy getting better, he got worse. Even when he came close to Jesus, the spirit said, "Ah, He needs to know that I am not turning you loose!" In other words, the devil grabbed all the harder. Anyone who has been addicted knows what this is about. Once a person makes a decision, the problem gets worse rather than better.

The Nature of Addictions. Addictions don't wave off like flies. Once an addiction has gotten into one's flesh, mind, nervous system, brain, feet and fingernails, from there it is a life and death struggle. The power of death, which has organized itself around this satanic power, and the power of grace are in warfare. It is not easy. The person pulls, then the addiction pulls back. An addiction can talk to a person like a natural man. It'll ask you, "What do you mean, letting go? You can't get along without me! You do what I say do." It will make you sweat. It will make you tremble.

Cocaine isn't the only addiction that talks like this. That little cigarette does too. Anyone who decides to deal with an addiction had better be ready for warfare.

In Mark the ninth chapter, they brought the demon-possessed boy to Jesus and when the spirit saw Jesus immediately it convulsed the boy. The boy fell on the ground and rolled around, foaming at the mouth. The father had said that it was a dumb spirit. However, he didn't mean that the spirit was actually dumb. The way the evil spirit manifested itself was to make the boy dumb. An addiction makes a person dumb. It takes one's voice and speaks its voice over the person's voice. Then the person has no power over his/her life. The person has no voice with respect to how he/she organizes his/her affections and desires. The spirit makes the person dumb.

However, there is another reason that the addiction is a dumb spirit. Notice back in Mark 9, that Jesus asks the father how long the boy had this spirit. Doctors take illnesses very seriously. In this passage, Jesus, the doctor, does a medical history. This was a different concept of healing than what is done in churches today. There was no "hocus pocus." In this passage, Jesus took time to do a medical history.

Most people involved in healing ministries don't want to do a diagnosis. They want instant cures. That is why many people go on with their addiction. They go on with addiction to religiosity. They go on with addictions to having a good time in church. They go on with addictions to emotionalism. Because the minister him/herself is addicted, s/he expects to heal these people in a hurry so that s/he can get back to his/her personal variety of addiction.

In Mark 9, we find that doubt itself is another addiction. When the father says, "I believe, help my unbelief," he is revealing an addiction to doubt. Doubt stands at the front door of grace. Grace is waiting to operate, but doubt stands in its way.

The Effects of Addiction. When Jesus saw that the crowd came running, He rebuked the uncleaned spirit. He said to it, "You dumb and deaf spirit." Recall that the father said it was merely a dumb spirit. Jesus corrected this because He had taken time to do a medical history. Jesus realized that this evil spirit had both a deaf and dumb manifestation. People who are addicted have lost their voices. That is what makes the addicted person dumb. However, the devil comes in and creates such a problem that the person can't hear the voice of grace inside.

The Voice of Grace. There is a voice inside of each person and the voice is speaking all of the time. It doesn't matter how low the person has gotten. This voice tells a person that s/he is someone. "You are the object of My love," God is saying, "you are My concern." However, addiction makes a person deaf to this voice. Addiction makes a person deaf and dumb. But God's voice is still saying, "You are My child. I don't care how low you go, My love will not turn you loose. I stand by you. I know you may have been down, ten times or fifteen times, but I am here to lift you up! Don't give up now! You belong to Me. Don't you see My trademark in your face? Don't you dare give up!"

Addictions can create so much confusion that a person can't hear this voice of Christ saying, "I love you."

The Role of Prayer. Recall that in Mark 9, Jesus said, "Come out of that man and don't go back inside of him anymore." Then the spirit cried and convulsed the boy again. It is a struggle. However, as a church we must help people to continue the struggle. They must know that, even if it doesn't seem to work the first time to try again. The church itself cannot become discouraged in its ministry to those who are addicted.

Recall that Jesus touched the boy. He took him by the hand and lifted him up. Afterwards, when the disciples were in the house, they asked, "Why were we unable to cast out the demons?" Jesus told them that the illness they were fighting could be conquered only by prayer and fasting.

The events of this scriptural passage occurred on the day that Jesus came down from the Mount of Transfiguration. His disciples were in a most embarrassing situation. A man had brought his son to Jesus in hopes that Jesus could heal him. But Jesus, Peter, James and John were on the mountaintop. This meant that the disciples who were left in the valley had to do something for this boy.

The Involvement of the Disciples. Can you hear them now? They are encountered by a crowd. People in the crowd are asking them where Jesus is. The disciples tell them that He is on a brief retreat. Then people complain, "Why is He always missing

67

when we need Him?" The disciples say, "He'll be back soon." Then they say, "Even if He were here what could He do?"

Then the disciples say, "He is able. He is a healer! We have seen it happen before." Then the people say, "Well, what about you guys? Aren't you all apprentices in His healing business? Didn't He give you the power to cast out devils?" Then can't you hear one of the scribes saying to the man whose son was standing there, "Turn your son over to them. They all are a part of this Christian enterprise. Let them try and see what they can do."

We're not told in the text what the disciples attempted to do. It is evident that they tried something. However, whatever it was, it had not worked. The disciples must have felt like preachers feel today when people in the streets ask, "What is your church doing about this drug problem? Aren't you all supposed to be in the business of uplifting the community? Can't your spiritual power confront this drug menace that is destroying this town?"

I can empathize with the disciples, because I have had similar experiences. I was once in a situation where I was trying to cast out some demons. It was at my father's church in Queens. They named it for him. It is Forbes Temple United Holy Church of America. Daddy had left me in charge while he had gone to a convocation.

That morning, a man walked through the doors of the church. He had on a vest and was dressed in a rather dirty, formal jacket. He came into the church and proceeded to take over. First he stood on the communion table. We all gathered around him to protect the honor of God. Then we tried our best to cast the demon out of the fellow.

We said, "Come out of him." We knew that if he was standing on the communion table, something was wrong with him. Then we began to try to do what we thought Jesus would do. We pointed our fingers and we began a chant, "Jesus, Jesus, Jesus." Then the man said, "You can talk about Jesus all you want, but I ain't goin' nowhere until I get ready."

Then he went up into the pulpit and said, "What you all need is some preaching." Then he proceeded to preach. We continued to say, "Jesus!" We prayed. We pleaded the blood of Jesus against him. We kept saying, "Come out of that man!" However, nothing happened.

Finally, an alert deacon went out and called the police. When the police came, they rushed to the back where the restroom was and flushed some quantities of cocaine down the stool. We found out that he was high and had some companions waiting there with him. Now every time I read this biblical text about the demon-possessed boy, it reminds me of drugs. It also causes me to identify with the disciples. I understand how embarrassed they felt, when they were not able to minister to this person who was possessed by a devil.

Today, the entire Christian church is in a state of embarrassment about this issue. That is why the topic of drugs is the subject of this chapter. The central question is: Is there any word from the Lord about drugs? If there is anything the churches must be able to do, if there's anything that the Gospel must do, my prayer is, Lord through us now, do it, even through this chapter. Bring the deliverance, if deliverance is possible. We stand Sunday after Sunday and proclaim the mighty power of God while people in the grip of addiction are hardly able to "keep on keeping on." I don't want Jesus to have to come down from the mountain and ask the people what happened. I don't want the people to say, "We brought our sons, our daughters, our mothers, our fathers, our cousins, our aunts, and our grandfathers to this church but they could not help."

Just as the people complained about Jesus being on retreat, they are now saying that the church is on retreat. Those who have drug problems are feeling somewhat self-conscious in the church. Perhaps they feel that they are the objects of our pity. They may hope that they will not be misunderstood, treated lightly, scolded, or given false hope. However, the problem is bigger than that. The problem is bigger than drug addiction. There are many types of addiction.

The Nature of the Problem. Therefore, the agenda for this chapter is larger than drug addiction. This is not a chapter that urges people to refuse prescribed medicines, used to sustain proper functioning of the body. That is not the intent of this chapter.

It is not about refusing medicine for high blood pressure or diabetes. It is not about throwing insulin away. It is not about throwing anti-seizure medicine away. It is not about throwing away anti-clotting materials that keep one's blood flowing at the proper consistency. It is not about throwing away medicine for glandular disorders. It is not about throwing away eye drops for glaucoma. This chapter does not urge anyone to be irresponsible regarding his/her health.

On the other hand, this chapter focuses on drug abuse. It focuses on the use of drugs that abuse the body, the mind, the spirit, the family and the community. The focus is not restricted to drug addiction. If we want Jesus to deal with people who are addicted to drugs, why not put all of our addictions on the altar.

The weakness surfaces like a boil. However, one must realize that the problem is deeper than this boil. The problem is that the whole body system itself has the capacity for self-destruction. There is an entire constellation of contributing causes. That is because we are in a network of relationships. That is why this chapter is for the entire church, not just for persons who may be addicted.

Gerald May in his book, *Addiction and Grace* begins with a fundamental conviction that all human beings have an inborn desire for God. It is a hunger to love, to be loved and to move closer to the source of love. May believes that this yearning is the essence of the human spirit. It is the origin of our highest hopes and our most noble dreams. He does not say that everyone is religious or that everyone is aware of this religious longing, but he believes that the need is fundamental to humankind.[2] There is that space in us that cries out for the One that is the source of our being. We are not going to be quite satisfied until that space has been entered by the divine being.

70

Some of us want to fill that space with something other than God. That leads to what has been called sin. Sin is what turns us away from love. It turns us away from love for ourselves, love for one another, and away from love for God.

One of the reasons that we repress our desire for love is that love makes us vulnerable to being hurt. We repress our desire for love to minimize suffering. When we repress our desire for love we cannot fill that space. The vacuum does not go away. It is when we repress our feelings that we set ourselves up for various kinds of addictions.

Addictions Attach to Desire. Addictions bond and enslave the energy of desire and cause certain behaviors that are designed to compensate for a sense of the absence of God in one's heart. Then the addiction to which we attach ourselves becomes a substitute or counterfeit love on our insides. However, it doesn't matter how much of the addictive substance a person gets, the person's longing for God is not satisfied.

Dr. May says that the psychological, neurological and spiritual dynamics of full-fledged addiction are actively at work within every human being. The same processes that are responsible for addictions to alcohol and narcotics are also responsible for addictions to outmoded ideas. The same processes produce workaholics, and produce people who are addicted to relationships.

Types of Addictions. Everyone is addicted. Some are addicted to power. Some are addicted to bad movies. Some are addicted to fantasies. In fact, May says that there are attraction addictions, and there are aversion addictions.

There are addictions to anger, approval, attractiveness, being good, being liked, being taken care of and eating. Other addictions involve the love of chocolates, gummy bears, coffee, toys, computers, depression, and alcohol. People with drug problems don't need to be singled out. There are plenty of other addictions.

71

What about people who are addicted to clothes? Have I reached your addiction yet? Other addictions include biting nails, and eating potato chips and pizza. Some people are addicted to revenge. Others are addicted to sex. Some are addicted to shoplifting, and others are addicted to sleeping. Some are addicted to soft drinks. Some are addicted to sports. Some are addicted to talking and some are addicted to watching television. Some folks are addicted to tobacco. Some folks are addicted to winning.

Some addictions can be classified as negative or aversion addictions. These are things a person cannot do. Such addictions include not being able to fly in an airplane. Others are afraid of being alone. Some young people are addicted to being discounted. That is why they say don't "dis me." Some people can't stand blood, snakes, bugs or closed-in spaces. Others can't stand commitment. Some people are negatively addicted to other races. Some are negatively addicted to rejection. Some are negatively addicted to success. Such people will fail when they are on the threshold of success because they are negatively addicted to success.

The Role of Idolatry. When a person becomes addicted, the person becomes an idolator. That is, the thing or substance to which the person becomes addicted usurps the space that only God should be filling. The person is an idolator because the person has something sitting on God's throne. However, it is not strong enough to heal or save the person, or give the person meaning or purpose. All an addiction can do is erode a person's free will. It eats away at one's dignity until one learns to hate oneself and others. It robs one of one's freedom. An addiction is antipathetic to love. An addiction prevents a person from being open to God's grace. That is why this chapter is designed for the whole church.

God and Addictions. Remember that, in Mark the ninth chapter, the scribes told the disciples that Jesus was gone, but the disciples said He was coming back, and when He came, He would handle the situation. Let us discover what Jesus did as described in Mark 9. First of all Jesus asked the people what was happening. He wanted to know what was happening in people's lives so that He could pray.

Today there is an entire generation that is "hyped up" on materialism, hedonism, and pleasure, first one type of addiction and then another. An entire generation has lost confidence in the power of Christ. The entire society is at fault and most of us are under attack by various addictions. We are living in a culture that has lost its relationship with the almighty God. Our culture no longer believes in the fact that we were made for God and that our hearts will be restless until we find rest in Jesus.

Returning to Mark 9, we see Jesus asking, "O faithless generation. How long am I to be with you?" Later on He asks the same question, "How long am I to bear with you?"

Then Jesus asks how long the young man has had the problem. Jesus is sensitive to time. It is important to recognize that one of the gifts of worship is the reminder to take time seriously. Time is serious. Time is running out. If some people don't "find themselves" soon it is uncertain what the future will be.

BIBLE STUDY APPLICATION

Instructions: The following exercises provide the opportunity to examine the story of the healing of the demon–possessed boy more closely. The first five exercises consist of five "discovery" questions and a summary question. The sixth exercise provides the opportunity to apply principles from this chapter to a church-based ministry. The seventh exercise is for personal application.

"And when he came to his disciples, he saw a great multitude about them, and the scribes questioning with them. And straightway all the people, when they be-

held him, were greatly amazed, and running to him saluted him. And he asked the scribes, What question ye with them? And one of the multitude answered and said, Master, I have brought unto thee my son, which hath a dumb spirit; And wherever he taketh him, he teareth him: and he foameth, and gnasheth with his teeth, and pineth away: and I spake to thy disciples that they should cast him out; and they could not. He answereth him, and saith, O faithless generation, how long shall I be with you? how long shall I suffer you? bring him unto me. And they brought him unto him: and when he saw him, straightway the spirit tare him; and he fell on the ground, and wallowed foaming. And he asked his father, How long is it ago since this came unto him? And he said, Of a child.

And ofttimes it hath cast him into the fire, and into the waters, to destroy him: but if thou canst do any thing, have compassion on us, and help us. Jesus said unto him, If thou canst believe, all things are possible to him that believeth. And straightway the father of the child cried out, and said with tears, Lord, I believe; help thou mine unbelief. When Jesus saw that the people came running together, he rebuked the foul spirit, saying unto him, Thou dumb and deaf spirit, I charge thee, come out of him, and enter no more into him. And the spirit cried, and rent him sore, and came out of him: and he was as one dead; insomuch that many said, He is dead. But Jesus took him by the hand, and lifted him up; and he arose. And when he was come into the house, his disciples asked him privately, Why could not we cast him out? And he said unto them, This kind can come forth by nothing, but by prayer and fasting" (Mark 9:14-29).

1. The Power of Faith

In Mark 9:23, Jesus said that everything is possible for the person who has faith.
a. What role did faith play in the creation of the world? (Hebrews 1:1-2; Genesis 1:1-8)
b. What role did faith play in life of the paralyzed man? (Matthew 9:1-7; Mark 2:1-12)
c. What role did faith play in the life of the woman with the issue of blood? (Matthew 19:18-22; Luke 8:40-48; Mark 5:21-32)
d. What role did faith play in helping blind people to see? (Mark 10:46-52; Matthew 15:29-31)
e. What role did faith play in the life of a parent dealing with a demon-possessed child? (Matthew 15:21-28)
f. SUMMARY QUESTION: What do all of these stories have in common? What role did faith play? What do these stories have in common with the story of the demon-possessed boy in Mark 9? Are there any implications for dealing with addictions today? Are there any guidelines from Dr. Forbes' sermon that apply?

2. The Power of Prayer

In Mark 9:29, Jesus says that only prayer can drive out evil spirits. Prayer is very powerful.
a. What was one manifestation of the power of prayer? (Acts 1:8; 2:1-4, 14-21, 37-41)
b. What was another manifestation of the power of prayer? (Acts 1:14-16; 2:1-4, 41, 42)

c. What was another manifestation of the power of prayer? (Acts 9:6, 20, 22)

d. What was still another manifestation of the power of prayer? (Acts 9:36-42)

e. What was yet another manifestation of the power of prayer? (Acts 12:1-18)

f. SUMMARY QUESTION: What do all of these stories have in common? What role did prayer play? How was the power of prayer manifested? What were the results? What implications are there for people suffering with addiction? What implications are there for relatives of people suffering with addictions? Are there any principles from Dr. Forbes' sermon that apply?

3. The Addiction to "Love"

The woman who met Jesus at the well had been married five times and was currently in an adulterous relationship (John 4:1-28).

a. On the surface, what type of thirst did the woman at the well have? (John 4:13-15)

b. Beneath the surface, in the seat of her emotions, what type of thirst did the woman have? (John 4:16-18)

c. How could the woman's thirst for love be quenched? (John 4:14)

d. What role would faith play? (Romans 3:21-24; 10:14-17)

e. What effect did Jesus' message have on this woman who was addicted to love? (John 4:25-29)

f. SUMMARY QUESTION: What does the Samaritan woman have in common with the demon-possessed boy of Mark 9? What does she have in common with people who are addicted to the quest for love today? Are there any guidelines from Dr. Forbes' sermon?

4. Addictions to Substances

Dr. Forbes made the point that many people try to fill their need for God with substances.

a. What effect did addiction have on Lot's life? (Genesis 19:30-38)

b. What effect did addictions have on Ben-Haddad's life? (1 Kings 20:1-11)

c. What effect did addictions have in Ahasuerus and Vashti's lives? (Esther 1:5-22)

d. What effect did substance abuse have in Adam and Eve's lives? (Genesis 1:15—3:8)

e. How does our Lord promise to deal with addictions? (John 6:30-40)

f. SUMMARY QUESTION: What do the people in these stories have in common? What do they have in common with the demon-possessed boy of Mark 9? What do they have in common with substance abusers today? Are there any principles from Dr. Forbes' sermon that apply?

5. Other Addictions

Dr. Forbes mentions various types of addictions. Some of these occur in people of the Bible.

a. What was Samson's addiction? (Judges 15:1-5, 6-8; 16:1-3, 21-30)

b. What were Ahaz and Jezebel's addictions? (1 Kings 16:29-33; 19:1-3; 2 Kings 21:1-15)

c. What was Herod's addiction? (Matthew 2:1-18; 14:1-12; 23:6-12)

d. What was the addiction of the man at the pool in Bethesda? (John 5:1-8)

e. What was Saul's negative addiction? (1 Samuel 16:14-15; 18:6-8; 19:1-2, 9-11)

f. SUMMARY QUESTION: What common types of effects

did addictions have in the lives of the characters (a-e)? Do they remind you of any people of today with similar types of addictions? Based on Dr. Forbes' sermon and the story in Mark 9, what is the ultimate solution for weakening the bondage to addictions?

6. CHURCH–BASED MINISTRY

Imagine that your church is either installing or attempting to improve a ministry to people who suffer from various addictions. What are the essential components of such a ministry? What should be taught? What supports should the church offer?

7. PERSONAL APPLICATION

Do you suffer with addictions? If so, re-read Dr. Forbes' sermon very carefully. Then take your addiction to God in prayer.

CHAPTER FOUR

Brenda and Ethel were sitting at the table, eating some potato chips and waiting for their husbands to come home. Both of their husbands worked at the same suburban factory. "Don't get too near that window," Brenda called to Stephanie, 10, who had run to the window to check on a noise she heard outside.

"Did they ever find out who shot those little boys the other day?" Ethel asked.

"I don't know. It's the third shooting this month. This place is getting to be like the Wild West. It didn't used to be that way," Brenda said.

"I don't know. I think it has something to do with the drug traffic. I keep telling you I believe there's a crack house down the street. You know they took the street signs down. I think that's a sign that someone has a crack house on the street," Ethel said.

"What is that noise coming from across the street, Ma?" Stephanie called.

"That's those church people leaving their prayer meeting," Brenda said. "Don't get too close to that window."

"You know, Brenda, when we were little, we used to laugh at those 'holy rollers,' remember?" Ethel asked.

"Yeah, I remember," recalled Brenda. "But you know, they seem like the only sane people on this

block. If it wasn't for them and Reverend Sanders, it wouldn't be no God nowhere around."

"Yeah, every time one of those fools kills somebody, that pastor's always right there, even if none of us go over to the church, except maybe on Easter Sunday, or with the kids or something," Brenda said.

There are many indications that African Americans respect and value the presence of the Black church, even though many may not attend it regularly, if at all. If one drove down any main street in nearly any Black community, one would notice many Black churches of various sizes and denominations.

There are very few reliable estimates of the percentages of Black people who are actual members of churches. However, the Committee on the Status of Black Americans, of the National Research Council presented one estimate in 1984. A random sample of 1,210 people were interviewed. Of the 157 African Americans in the sample, 57.3% attended church, compared to 42.9% of the 1,053 whites who were interviewed.[1] However, this sample is much too small to make any generalizations from it.

In a more recent study (1991) by Lincoln and Mamiya, out of a random nationwide sample of 2,150 Black church representatives interviewed, an average of 390 people per church were on the membership rolls, with an average of 479 members for urban churches. In the same population of Black churches, 13% reported more than 600 members, and 26.8% reported having 200-599 members.[2]

As encouraging as these figures may sound, there are still those who disregard the presence of a physical church—the symbol of God's presence in the community—and ignore God's people. People who establish crack houses within the vicinity of places where God's people gather for worship are examples of people with this attitude.

In the following sermon, Dr. William Pannell reminds us of a time in the history of Israel, when both its leaders and its people disrespected the Ark of the Covenant (the symbol of God's presence among His people), and the rules by which God asked His people to live. They were on the brink of genocide and would have perished were it not for the Lord being on their side but the Lord's mercy. Pannell draws parallels between those times and ours, and calls African Americans back to a respect and a response to the presence of God among them.

GENOCIDE, SURVIVAL, OR VICTORY?

Dr. William Pannell
1 Samuel 4:19-22

The title does not assume that every African American is either a victim of genocide or is merely surviving. Some people are triumphant. Not everything about them is bad news. For these types of people the goal of surviving is passé. They have moved beyond survival, to living.

On the other hand, there are some very hard choices to be made in the near future. Many African Americans in this great country have watched their options diminish to the point where the question of suicide, genocide or survival really is an important issue. It is not just a physical issue, but a spiritual one. It is an intellectual, moral and psychological issue. It is this way for a significant number of Americans who are living at the margins. Some have lost even that and are just barely "out there."

National magazines which have nothing to do with being Black, increasingly are highlighting the plight of various sectors of the Black community, focusing on Black young boys and Black young men.

The Status of Minorities. People living as minorities within their cultures are always in jeopardy. The Children of Israel were such a people, and they were always in jeopardy. They still are. This is true of any group of people, anywhere in the world, in all of history, who by their relative numbers within a dominant culture are a minority. Any people when relatively powerless (even if, as in the case of South Africa, their numbers are larger than that of those who oppress them), are in jeopardy. Powerless people are always in peril. They are always flipping around the edges of the question, "What is before us, genocide or survival?"

One can compare different groups within a particular minority group. However, minorities, who tend to be relatively powerless, are always in jeopardy. Other minorities, who may have power and who may have their own destiny within their own confines, may have put themselves in jeopardy by using immoral practices to obtain power.

The Case of Israel. However, for Israel the future was not determined by the Amalekites and the Jebusites. The issue of what Israel was going to be was not to be decided by her enemies. The issue of what Israel was going to be was to be decided by Israel!

In one of the most pointed stories in the Bible, a woman gives birth to a child and, whereas that is usually an occasion for rejoicing, this time it was the occasion for sorrow, heaviness and disaster. The woman had received news that her husband was dead. She had discovered that the armies of God had been beaten on the battlefield and that the Ark of the Covenant of God, that great symbol of the Lord's presence among His people, had been taken away by the enemy.

Then her labor pains came upon her and she gave birth to a baby boy. Ordinarily this ought to have been an incredible moment for rejoicing in this Jewish family. Instead, the woman sensed that there was a significance and symbolism of this boy, born in the midst of what had occurred. She had given birth to life in the midst of death. A whole society had died. Therefore, she named the child Ichabod. She realized that the glory of God had taken wings like a grieved dove and had flown away.

The Absence of the Ark of the Covenant. Take a look at this. It is very easy to see. The outline is here. This is a wonderful passage of Scripture. The glory of God symbolized by the Ark of the Covenant, has departed from Israel's religious life. The Israelites did not mourn because some preachers were killed. They mourned because the Ark of the Covenant was taken away. That symbol of God's presence had been taken away. The enemy had captured that marvelous piece of furniture.

However, every place that the Ark went outside of Israel, the judgment of God fell upon whoever had it. God could take care of Himself. Seemingly God was out there almost all alone. He had no people and no priest to bear the Ark. However, God doesn't need help. God is quite capable of being God without anyone—whether in grace or in judgment.

The Question of Leadership. The problem with God, of course, is that He always wants to surround Himself with a people. God always seeks after a people among whom He can dwell. He founded a people out of Abraham and Sarah, Isaac and that whole, marvelous prodigy of men and women. The family of God was never happier. It was never more content. It was never more blessed than when God was among His people and His people loved and obeyed God. God was happy.

However, Israel decided, through its leadership, that it was not content. Israel was unable to rise above its leadership. Its leadership was aging. Eli, the old prophet, was 95 years old. He was blind, and he couldn't hear too well. He couldn't get around much anymore. When he heard the news that Israel had been defeated, it shocked him. He fell over backwards and broke his neck. In another day he might have survived. He might have fallen and perhaps braced himself. He might have twisted and suffered only a broken rib. However, on that day he just falls over and dies.

Israel's leadership was being replaced by a younger leadership which did not know the Lord. The Bible says they were sons of the devil. That is a terrible thing to be said about any group of people. But it is really terrible when that is said about a people who are priests of God, and who have the office of the ministry, who stand before the altar, who represent God before the people. It was said about these people. They were called the sons of the devil who knew not God. Any group of people who are called to follow such a leadership is in serious trouble.

These evil leaders did not regard the Lord's offering. They treated God's offering and God's people with contempt. They stood before the altars of God and shook their little clay fists into the face of our Lord. They said "nuts" to all the redemptive programs of God. They were in it for what they could get out of it. That was the quality of leadership that came to the land, a leadership that knew not the Lord.

Having poor leadership is not a new problem. Historically people of God have been cursed with poor leaders who, for some sick reason, became involved in the work of God. Most had selfish, carnal, and sinful reasons. One evidence of their motives is that they wanted theirs first. However, they set it up in such a way that it didn't appear that way. They got little servants. They found others to do the work for them.

Another problem these men had is that they liked women. Who doesn't? The problem was that these guys were already married. The woman in the Bible who bore the son in the midst of death and saw her child die in childbirth, had known for years that her husband had been "shacking up" with other women. Those women were in the house of God! She'd known it for years. It appears that everyone knew it. Even the old man Eli knew that his sons had made themselves vile before God. Instead of being holy, these guys were "horny."

84

Glory departed from Israel's religious life primarily because Israel's leadership did not take God seriously. Glory even departed from Israel's family life.

This Israelite woman gave birth to a child and the child was an orphan on the day he was born. When a society does not make room for God in its national life, or even in its religious life, its families produce generation after generation of orphans. They produce young people who have no focus, no purpose, no bearing, no sense of who they are, no sense of where they are, no sense of where they ought to go and no sense of how to get there. They're just out there! They are orphans.

Today's Leadership. A PBS documentary carried a story about a young man who sold himself on the streets. The young man was being destroyed, not so much by the life he lived, but by anger and frustration. A person could see it in his face, hear it in his voice, and listen to it in his language. The young man said, "I don't know what the hell life is all about, but I sure as hell don't want to die." It sounded like being between a rock and a hard place. If this young man didn't know what life was all about, he was already dead before he got AIDS. How could he find out what life is about? Through his parents? Through his church? Through the holy men and women of God? They are the ones who would teach him the ways of the Lord, and the ways of the Lord are life.

There are so many young people out there who are cut off from their families and communities. The only way they are surviving is by forming communities of lost boys and girls, men and women. These communities have become communities of the lost and the damned.

Returning to Israel, recall that glory had departed from the family. It had departed from Israel's political life. If a people "thumb their noses" at God at any level, it is bound to affect their politics. Ultimately it will corrupt the national leadership.

That is the type of leadership that emerges when people exorcise God out of their culture. That was what was going on among the Israelites. They were in a situation in which the Philistines didn't know what to do when the Ark of the Covenant was brought into the camp of the Israelites. The Israelites saw the Ark of the Covenant just before the great day of battle. They heaved up a great shout. The Ark of the Covenant was a symbol of their God among them one more time. The Philistines knew they couldn't win, because the Israelites' God was with them.

The Philistines discovered that the Israelites had the symbol of God's presence, but their culture had thumbed its nose at God and walked away. God really wasn't there. Therefore, Israel got wiped out. That even surprised Israel's enemies.

The moral of all of this is that God can take care of Himself. However, He wants to find a people who will take Him seriously. Whatever happens among so-called minority peoples is going to be determined by what they themselves will to make happen. It will all depend upon whether they take God seriously.

Today, thousands of years later, leadership is still in trouble. All kinds of men in the ministry have left the ministry. It's not because they despise God. They just got busy doing things that are not at the core and heart of ministry. They have no prayer life. They are too busy to pray. These are men who regard prayer as important, but they are not men who seek the face of God. They are not men whose lives are centered in God at the depth of their being. This is not to say that these men have not had seminary training. This is not to say that they are not gifted.

It is to say that, at the core of their beings, where ministry begins, God is not there. In fact, very frequently, these are leaders who know not the Lord. It is possible to be busy with ministry but not to know the Lord. Whenever that is the case, the people whom a leader is called to serve are in jeopardy.

Eli's sons knew not the Lord. They despised the offering, despised the Lord, and despised the people of God. They had not been converted.

The Need and Nature of Conversion. Conversion is radical. It doesn't have much to do with how tall, short, fat or slim a person is. It has nothing to do with what type of car a person drives. It doesn't have much to do with cigars, cigarettes or tiparillos, like people once thought it did.

Conversion has something to do with whether there has been a change in the heart, in the core of one's very being. Conversion is like being born again. It is radical. Being born again is radical. It occurs when God, who commanded the light to shine out of darkness, shines into a human heart and pierces the inky darkness of the person's pagan heart, flooding it with light.

In this moment God implants, in the soil of the heart which is dead, sudden life which explodes. God, the liberator comes to the prison house where men and women are in bondage to sin and sets them free. Their chains fall off. They fly away with fresh wings, with strength and glory into sunlight.

Conversion is very radical. If a person is going to follow leadership in the name of God, one of the things that the person would want of the leadership, is that the leaders are converted. In both the Old and New Testaments, the conversion which God produces is always expressed in ethical conduct. A person cannot be converted to God and live as the person pleases. A converted person must change.

Where to Begin. The responsibility does not lie with the people in the suburbs. Where does one start? One must start with prayer. One must also start with repentance and confession. That is, what is meant by conversion? By doing this, a person lets God know that s/he knows He can take care of Himself, but that s/he would like to be partners with Him in His business.

In the midst of Israel's crisis, God illustrated this. God illustrated this when He found Himself a boy, a boy child. To do this, He first found Himself a woman. He found a woman by the name of Hannah, who gave God back a boy child. At the time, the boy was just a child. However, God taught that child. He did not leave Himself without a witness.

If African Americans pay the dues to God that God requires, God will use them just as He used Samuel to bring a people back to Himself. If African Americans come back to God, African Americans can get their children back. They can get their families back together, and they can get godly leadership at every level of the community.

BIBLE STUDY APPLICATION

Instructions: The following exercises provide the opportunity to study 1 Samuel 4:19-22 more closely. The first five exercises consist of five "discovery" questions and a summary question. The sixth exercise asks you to apply the knowledge gained in this chapter to a church-based ministry. The seventh exercise allows for personal application.

"And his daughter-in-law, Phinehas' wife, was with child, near to be delivered: and when she heard the tidings that the ark of God was taken, and that her father-in-law and her husband were dead, she bowed herself and travailed; for her pains came upon her. And about the time of her death the women that stood by her said unto her, Fear not; for thou hast borne a son. But she answered not, neither did she regard it. And she named the child I-chabod, saying, The glory is departed from Israel: because the ark of God was taken, and because of her father-in-law and her husband. And she said, The glory is departed from Israel: for the ark of God is taken" (1 Samuel 4:19-22).

1. Environment in Which Phinehas' Widow Lived

The widow of Phinehas lived in an unstable political environment (1 Samuel 4:19).

a. What role did Hophne and Phinehas (the widow's husband) play? (1 Samuel 1:1-3)

b. What type men were Hophne and Phinehas? (1 Samuel 2:12-17)

c. Specifically, what was the general political situation in which the widow had been living, and how might this have affected family life? (1 Samuel 2:22-25)

d. What prophecies had been made concerning Eli's family? (1 Samuel 2:27-36)

e. What parts of the prophecy concerning Eli's family had come true? (1 Samuel 4:1-18)

f. SUMMARY QUESTION: In what ways could the behavior of the religious leaders of 1 Samuel 1—4 have led to the extinction of the Israelites (if it had not been for the Lord on their side)? Are there any warnings in this passage for African Americans or any other Christians of today?

2. The Nature of Hophne and Phinehas' Disrespect

Hophne and Phinehas, sons of Eli and religious leaders, did not appear to respect God's laws regarding sacrificial offerings (4:19).

a. What procedures had God given to Moses, in the Mosaic Law, regarding animal sacrifices? (Leviticus 3:1-5, 16; 7:30-34; 3:1-5, 16)

b. Why were sin offerings made? (Leviticus 4:1-2; 5:1-6, 15) Of what significance was burning off the fat? (4:20, 26, 31, 35; 5:10)

c. What did Hophne and Phinehas do? (1 Samuel 2:12-16)

d. What effect were sin offerings to have? (Leviticus 12:8; 14:20; 16:19)

e. Why do we no longer need to make animal sacrifices for sin? (Hebrews 13:8-16; 3:1-2; 4:14-15; 5:1-10; 7:15—8:13)

f. SUMMARY QUESTION: Reread 1 Samuel 4:19-22. In your opinion, what was the relationship between the disrespect for the sin offering and the people's vulnerability to defeat? In your opinion, do people take sin lightly today? What effect could it have on a community's survival?

3. The Presence of God and the Survival of Community

The Ark of the Covenant symbolized God's presence among the families of Israel. It had a long and significant history among them (4:21-22).

a. From where did the idea for the Ark of the Covenant come, and where was it kept? What was the covenant that was involved? (Exodus 25:8-22; 40:16-21)

b. When the Children of Israel traveled from Sinai, where God gave them sacred instructions, what role did the Ark of the Covenant play? What memories were associated with it? What effect did it have on community life? (Numbers 10:11-36)

c. When the Children of Israel crossed the Jordan under the leadership of Joshua, what role did the Ark of the Covenant play and what effect did it have on community life? (Joshua 3, 4)

d. In the Battle of Jericho, what role did the Ark of the Covenant play, and what effect did it have on community life? (Joshua 6:1-20)

e. What role did the presence of the Ark of the Covenant play in the life of Samuel, the leader God raised to take the place of Eli's evil sons? (1 Samuel 1:19-20, 24-28; 2:18-20; 3:1-21)

f. SUMMARY QUESTION: Considering these stories from Israel's history, summarize the effect that God's presence (represented in the Ark of the Covenant) had on community survival. What role has God's presence (represented in the Black Church) had on the survival of the Black community?

4. The Death of Phinehas' Widow

The sudden capture of the Ark of the Covenant containing the tablets of the Mosaic Law, along with the deaths of her husband and father-in-law, had more than one meaning for Phinehas' widow (4:19-22).

a. Within the Mosaic Law, what is one way that the community cared for the needy (including widows)? (Deuteronomy 14:22-29; 15:1-11; 26:12-15)

b. According to the Mosaic Law, what is another way that the community cared for the needy? (Deuteronomy 24:19-22)

c. According to the Mosaic Law, what provisions were made so that widows (and/or women without men) could have fellowships? (Deuteronomy 16:13-15; Leviticus 23:33-43)

d. According to the Mosaic Law, what provisions were made for a widow's remarriage? (Deuteronomy 25:5-10)

e. What assurances are there that the widow was mistaken— God's presence cannot be permanently removed from among His people! (Jeremiah 31:15-22)

f. SUMMARY QUESTION: Considering a-d, what are some reasons for the widow's strong emotional reaction to the news of the capture of the Ark of the Covenant? Compare the role that the Community of Faith (gathered around the Ark of the Covenant) had in the life of the widow, with the role that the church has played in the survival of husbandless African American women raising children.

5. God's Presence

God's presence never left Israel permanently. God's Spirit has always remained among God's people, working toward the goal of the survival and victory of the human community.

a. What effect can the Spirit of God have on the enemies of God's people? (1 Samuel 5:1—6:6)

b. Explain the role that repentance plays in the presence of God's Spirit in the lives of His people. (1 Samuel 6:7—7:2)

c. How was the Ark of the Covenant eventually returned to Jerusalem? (2 Samuel 6:1-15) What role did repentance play? (2 Samuel 6:13)

d. Eventually the Ark of the Covenant was placed in the temple constructed by Solomon in Jerusalem. Then the temple became the symbol of God's presence among His people. Eventually, what happened to the temple and to the Ark of the Covenant? (2 Kings 24:8-16) How was the temple rebuilt? (Ezra 6:3, 13-19)

e. After its initial destruction, the temple was rebuilt. But the Ark of the Covenant symbolizing the presence of God, was not there. Eventually, how did God manifest Himself among His people? (John 1:1-18; Acts 1:1-9; 2:1-21; Hebrews 13:5)

f. SUMMARY QUESTION: Today, the question is often raised as to whether African Americans will survive, as a group, into the 22nd century. Considering your answers to a-e, how would you answer this question?

6. CHURCH–BASED MINISTRY

Make a list of specific ways in which your local church can assume a leadership role in the survival and victory of the community surrounding your church.

7. PERSONAL APPLICATION

Consider your answer to #6. Make a list of ways that you can have a personal impact on your church and help to move it into its role of community renewal, survival and victory.

CHAPTER FIVE

Ron, a jurist, sat in the jury box, staring at the thir-teen–year–old boy who was on trial for murder. The court was nearly silent as the boy was being ques-tioned by his court–appointed defense attorney.

The boy described to the court how he had been bul-lied by several of the boys in his neighborhood for nearly a year. They just didn't like him, the boy had said, because he wouldn't join their gang, and he wouldn't run drugs for them.

"It had gotten so bad that he couldn't go to school or come home without his grandfather. His grandfather was around, because he is retired now," his mother told the court in her testimony. "We had to watch him at all times. I don't know what we would have done if it hadn't been for his grandfather."

"I couldn't leave the house. I couldn't even go to the store, without them cornering me and taking my money," the boy told the court, as the members of the jury listened. "I just got tired of it," he continued. "One day, I decided that I was going to sneak out when my grandfather wasn't looking. I wasn't gonna be locked up all of the time. But I knew that I couldn't go out unless I took a gun to protect me."

"Where did you get the gun?" the defense attorney asked.

"I got it from the closet where my grandfather kept it," he answered.

"Then what did you do?" the attorney asked.

"I went down to the playground, and when I got there, Dennis and his friends started messing with me again," the boy answered.

"What do you mean when you say 'messing with me'?" asked the attorney.

"They kept pushing me and laughing, and calling me names," he answered.

"What happened then?" the attorney asked.

"I lost control of myself. My whole body got hot, and I was trembling. Then I reached for the gun in my pocket and shot him," the boy said, with a trembling voice, as a tear made its way down his cheek.

He described how the other boys ran away, and how he left Dennis on the ground to die. By the time he reached his home, the police were there.

Ron, the jurist, listened as the defense attorney argued that the boy had signed a confession before getting proper legal advice, and that the people assigned to help him had essentially ignored him while he was awaiting trial. She argued that the boy's actions be considered as self-defense.

As Ron listened, it became plain to him that the boy was a victim of an evil world system over which he had no control. It almost seemed as though there was a conspiracy against him. It was as if Satan himself had begun attacking the boy through his friends and now had the boy where he wanted him. As the story *was told, there didn't seem to be any way out for the boy, from beginning to end.*

Unfortunately, the boy in this case study is only one of thousands of young Black men who tell similar stories to similar courts every day throughout the United States. Moreover, based on these and similar current trends, sociologists and others are predicting that the Black male is an "endangered species." For example, the most recent vital statistics present a life expectancy of Black men of 65.2 compared to a life expectancy of 69.4 for Black people in general, and 75.6 for white people in general.[1]

In March, 1991, the National Center for Health Statistics released figures estimating that 48% of Black males ages 15-19, who are killed, die from gunshot wounds, compared to only 18% for white males.[2] On the weekend of 9/11/90 alone, in Chicago, at least 75 shooting incidents were reported to police, resulting in 13 deaths. And in one weekend of August, 1991 in the same city, there were at least 35 shooting deaths involving Black men.[3]

In January, 1992, 77 murders were committed in Chicago. Most of these involved Black people, with Black men as the most common victims. The U.S. Department of Justice, in June, 1989, reported that 90.8 per 1,000 Black boys between the ages of 12 and 15 reported being victims of violent crimes (compared to 65.7 per 1,000 for white males).[4] The figure is 101 per thousand for Black boys between the ages of 16-19 (compared to 89.4 for white boys in the same age group). In nearly every age range, the number of Black men reporting that they are victims of violence is higher than the rate for white men.[5]

Moreover, in a 1986 study, it was found that, when population differences are taken into account, the number of Black men who

95

are incarcerated is 4.5 times that of whites. When individual states are taken into account, it is even higher. For example, in Illinois, the incarceration rate is 15 times that of whites and in Michigan, it is 13 times that of whites.[6]

Other factors are also threatening the survival of the Black male. These include sexually transmitted diseases. While the current syphilis rate is now 20 cases per 100,000 people (an increase of 82% since 1985), the rate for Black men is 156 per 100,000 compared to 116 for Black women, three for white males, and two for white females.[7] *Regarding AIDS, the Center for Disease Control reports that, while African Americans constitute about 12% of the general American population, about 27% of the estimated AIDS cases are African American, and the CDC estimates that 90% of all cases are males.*[8]

Taken together, these facts had led many to believe that there is a conspiracy to destroy Black men—a conspiracy that is, to a large extent, outside of their control. In the following article, Tom Skinner explores the notion of the conspiracy, and he provides spiritual guidelines for reversing these negative trends in the Black community.

THE AFRICAN AMERICAN MALE

Tom Skinner
1 Corinthians 13

Let's examine 1 Corinthians chapter 13. The 13th verse of 1 Corinthians 13 says, "Now abideth faith, hope, love, these three, but the greatest of these is love."

Those three words—faith, hope, love—in the last verse of the

13th chapter of Corinthians are three facets of the same idea that God is teaching in this passage. In fact, faith, hope and love appear together quite often. In Hebrews 2, the writer says that faith is the substantiation, the proving of things hoped for, the evidence of things not seen. It is not by accident that, in the 13th chapter of Corinthians, the words faith, hope and love are tied to the future.

Scripture always rivets us toward the future. In fact, all of Scripture is future-oriented. That is because God wants us to be goal-oriented. He wants us to constantly examine the Scriptures that remind us of that. He advises us not to go to the left or to the right, but to press toward the mark of the prize of the high calling which is in Christ. That pressing is always a pull toward the future.

The past is important only if one can learn from it. There is a funny thing about the head. The body tends to go in the direction that the head is pointing. If a person is constantly looking backwards, the body has to slow down. That is why coaches tell track stars that they must never look back. It is dangerous to look back even to see where the people you are running against are, because your body has to slow down in order to look back at them. God always wants our direction to take us forward.

Faith. Faith itself is about the future. Faith is about the expectation of what we believe God is going to do. Hope is about the future. Hope is about the belief that no matter how dark things are that God is going to make them all right. It is the confidence that God is going to do what He said He was going to do. Hope moves a person forward.

Hope. The hope of any generation is in its children. The hope of the future is in what we produce for the future. However, we must consider the fact that time is different with God than it is with human beings. The science of time is fascinating. Consider that the closer a person gets to the speed of light, the more time compresses.

97

Remember that the Bible refers to God as light. Light travels 186 thousand miles per second. It travels around the circumference of the earth 3 1/2 times in one second. Astronauts tell us that when they are in orbit at 25,000 miles an hour, on one side of the window, they can look out and see sunset and on the other side of the window, they can see sunrise. That is because as they increase in speed, time compresses. In the mind of God it was only yesterday that Jesus died on the cross. God, because of who He is, has the ability to see sunrise and sunset, the beginning and ending of history at the same time.

However, God always thinks of the future. The present and the past don't matter that much. God has decided that, for the sake of future generations, hope rests with our children. The question remains, what in our children signals hope?

The Endangered Species. There is a sign of desperation in the future, when we consider the male children of our communities, particularly African American boys. They are an endangered species. If Black males were compared with other species, they would be declared by an act of Congress to be endangered.

The question we face is: How do we protect our future? What is the role of those of us in the body of Christ who have been called upon to educate the children from the perspective of the kingdom of God? In other words, when we teach a class, speak the Word of God or try to impart knowledge about God, we must always be aware that there is an African American male sitting out there, whose chances of survival are small.

Consider the fact that, out of seven young boys in your church under the age of 10, one of them is expected to be gone by the time he is 12 years old. Two of them are expected to be gone by the time they are 16. It is possible that by the time the seven boys reach 30 years of age, only three of them may be alive. That is because the Black male is an endangered species.

The Conspiracy. Their endangerment is also because a conspiracy exists. It is against Black male leaders, and it is for the very life blood of young African American men. What does the conspiracy look like? *Webster's Dictionary* tells us that a conspiracy is an illegal meeting, generated by a group of lawless people to bring about destruction somewhere. Such a conspiracy is taking place in urban centers throughout our nation. It is against our children—particularly our male children.

No race of people can survive without males. In Scripture whenever the enemy wanted to move against the people of God, he always threatened to kill the male children. Pharaoh did this in Egypt. Herod did this in Jesus' time. The process of elimination begins at birth.

Babies Having Babies. It begins with children having children. It begins with little girls walking down the street sucking their thumbs holding onto their babies. This is the destruction and the conspiracy. A child who still needs to be raised becomes a child responsible for raising a child. By the time this child reaches 21, her child is six years old. Then the mother discovers that she missed being a teenager. Now she wants to be a teenager again.

In seeking to return to the teen years, she neglects her child. Perhaps the child is burned in a fire because Mama is not around. The conspiracy is further implemented when the father is also nowhere to be found.

This problem is nowhere more graphically illustrated than it was in a documentary broadcast on PBS. The program dealt with pregnant teens in Newark, New Jersey. It began with a young girl sitting among other young girls, all of whom had given birth to children but were unmarried. They were talking about men with disdain, anger and bitterness.

One girl said, "My mama didn't need no man. I don't need no man. My child won't need no man." At 19 years of age, this young mother was pregnant with her fifth child. The reporter asked her, "Young lady, wouldn't you want the father of these children to assist you in educating them?" These were her exact words: "Naw, 'cause him is pitiful. Him can't take care of himself."

Then the reporter asked, "Why do you keep relating to him then and having children by him, if he is so pitiful?" This was her exact response: "I suppose it's because I have a weakness for bow-legged boys."

In other words, the extent of the attraction was his bowed legs. They melted her. However, the male image that was needed to impact her child's life was nowhere to be found. Then the reporter went to interview the boy to whom this woman referred. This guy had his shades on in the dark and was trying to be real cool. When the reporter asked him about being responsible, he said, "Listen man, that's not my responsibility. She came up pregnant. She laid down and came up pregnant. Any woman I relate to, I let it be known that if they get pregnant, it's on them."

Here was a young man who had no sense of responsibility. He had no understanding of the sacredness of sex. He had no sense of the responsibility of it. He understood nothing about fatherhood. He had fallen through the cracks in life. There may have been a day in which that young woman or that young man were exceptions to the rule. However, that is no longer true. This is now the rule.

The Absence of the Wisdom of the Elders. At one time, uncles, grandmothers, grandfathers and aunties took the children of these children in. For example, when I was eight years old I was fortunate enough for all four of my grandparents to still be alive. I had the privilege of growing up on the backside of a generation of older people. When I was eight years old my grandparents ranged in age between 72 and 76. That was a norm for my time.

However, now we are faced with a generation in which a young father is not even a senior in high school, and his grandmother is under 45. The time to acquire wisdom in the family has shrunk. The wisdom that simply comes with age is not there anymore. There are no old people in many Black young people's lives. So the conspiracy moves on.

Poverty, Ignorance, and Disease. Then the child, born in these circumstances, faces other problems: poverty, which leads to malnutrition; ignorance, due to a lack of education; inability to acquire marketable skills. The ability to build an immune system to fight off disease is weakened due to malnutrition. The parents, due to lack of education, do not know the proper food to put into the child's body. Four–year–old children drink coca-cola for breakfast and eat potato chips for lunch. No one talks to them about vitamins, minerals and proteins. The child who has had the child doesn't know about these things. The older people who once imparted this wisdom are not around.

Child Deaths. Therefore the child's chances of survival are lessened. As a consequence, the death rate for male children is now high. In Harlem, it is higher than almost any community in the world. There, the number of child deaths now exceeds child deaths in Bangladesh, India. The conspiracy continues.

Children who survive reach 12 years of age. However, between eight and twelve years of age, male children die as innocent victims of violence. They are not necessarily participants in fights. Often they are innocent victims, hit by stray bullets while playing in the streets. They are hit by crossfires between gangs over territory. The minute a child reaches 12 years of age his chances of becoming a victim automatically increase. This time his mortality is linked to drug traffic.

The Role of Organized Crime. The part of the conspiracy related to drugs began at the end of World War II, around 1946. At that time, syndicated crime did not want to become involved with drugs. It wanted to concentrate on illegal liquor, prostitution, gambling, and other forms of revenue. However, the new crime families which were just developing at the close of World War II have reached the point where they must get involved with drugs and gang fights.

They have begun to take over the illegal drugs industry. Ganglords have now begun fighting over the distribution of drugs. By the end of 1948, syndicated crime agreed that, in order to keep gang killings low, syndicated crime would allow the distribution of drugs, but confine it to the Black communities of America. According to the movie "The Godfather" that was an actual agreement! The distributions could only be made in Black communities of America! Then began the introduction of heroin, from heroin to cocaine, and from cocaine to its lethal form of crack, and God only knows what the new formula will have to be once bodies become accustomed to the old drugs.

Now syndicated crime has decided that they want to control all drug distribution. They have decided to create a distribution center from which to distribute drugs all over the country to grassroot communities.

Although syndicated crime likes to control everything it does, it cannot produce fungus fast enough to implement what they hope to do. Therefore they have decided that they need enforcers.

The Involvement of Gangs. Beginning about five years ago, there was a tremendous multiplication of gangs in the United States. Gangs have expanded something like 120 to 130 times in cities all over America. Individually, they are smaller than they were before, and the syndicate is now using these gangs to control the drugs. The gangs are being used to enforce distribution. If someone gets "out of line," it is the job of the gang to keep the person in line. Many of the gang fights in Los Angeles, Detroit and New York are the results of people fighting, not over gang control, but over gang distribution of drugs. That is why our children are dying. The conspiracy continues.

Crack is causing our young men to drop in the streets. With these violent assaults, a large number of our young men are dead before they reach 16 years of age. Given the babies having babies, given the health problems that kill children young, given the innocent victims of violence, given the violence of gang warfare, given the drug distribution and given the drug usage itself, more young men will die. The number of young men will diminish by the time they reach the age of 16. Then between 18 and 30, tremendous devastation starts to take place in our cities.

Young Women in Crisis. Given these realities, it is a challenge to raise Christian girls with a hope for marriage. My daughters told me, a few years ago, that if they took the brothers who are on drugs, and put them aside as ineligible, and then took the brothers who are incarcerated, and put them aside, and then took the brothers who have decided not to be brothers, but sisters, and put them aside, from among those that are remaining, they have the challenge of locating a man who loves God and is filled with the Holy Ghost. They must locate one who understands what it means to be the husband of one wife, and who wants to be the father of children, and who wants to be a priest in his home, from among this group. They told me that I must be joking if I expected them to avoid dating unsaved men.

One of my daughters is now 24 years old. She went out and adopted a nine–month–old baby, because she was unsure whether there would be any brothers around to afford her the opportunity to be a mother in the normal way. That illustrates the desperation of the situation. The conspiracy has eliminated an entire generation of men who are available. However, there is still the challenge of preaching the Good News. There is still the challenge of raising a body of believers who love God.

The kingdom of God is in trouble in our neighborhoods. Yet another generation is being wiped out. God did not intend for this unbalanced situation to be. God had a definite plan in mind when He made man and woman, and said that the two should become one. God had something in mind when He ordained families. He did not intend for the situation to be warped, as it is today. The situation is so desperate now that when one gets into that 18 to 30 age category, the homicide rate goes up, the drug rate goes up, the violence builds up, and the number of men dying in that age range is greater than the number of children being born.

When Black women talk about Black men, they cannot escape some responsibility for some of this. Those boys are some sisters' brothers. Those boys are some sisters' sons. We are tied

103

in this thing together. At a conference at Howard University, a group of Black women arrived at several strategies for survival of Black women in the 21st century: (1) change sexual preferences, (2) date men of other cultures and races, (3) cope with being alone, and (4) share men. That is how some of our women define the situation. The conspiracy continues.

Symbols and Language. What is interesting is the language of young men. Nothing is sacred anymore. There is a whole generation with a different language. Words like "waste" are used for killing. Taking a person's life is like pouring water down a drain. It is like spilling milk. I have observed this when I have been asked to do eulogies. At one funeral, people came down to look at the casket during the wake the night before the funeral. Some of the members of the gang stood off to the side. Every few minutes, some people would come down the aisle, give one another a "high five" signal and laugh.

When the funeral service was over, the casket was taken out and put in a limousine. Again, they slapped a "high five" signal. After this happened a second, third and fourth time, it dawned on me that for them, the funeral was the epitome of life. Life was so dingy, so unsacred, so uncertain and so terrible that the funeral was their height of recognition! What they were seeing was that no one knew Joe existed while he was alive. They would look at him coming, and they would slap a high five. Today Joe lay in the casket. His suit was pressed. He had on a shirt and a tie, and he looked cool. They drove him away in a limousine, and for the first time, Joe was riding high. That's how distorted life had become for them. There seemed to be no hope. The conspiracy plot thickens.

A Profile of "Joe," Part of the Endangered Species. When young men such as "Joe" start school in the first grade, 48% of them will not reach the 12th grade. Fewer yet will ever get a diploma. For every 100 of them that enter the 9th grade in high school, only 19 of them will graduate. Of the 19 who get diplomas, most will read, write and compute at the fourth grade level. Most will have gone through a school system that just

104

"puts the child through." Such schools demand nothing more than that he attend every day. That is how the state and federal money keeps flowing. The fact that Joe doesn't learn anything doesn't matter. The school just pushes him through. Such young men have no skill to put bread on anyone's table. The conspiracy thickens.

Competition from Immigrants. Another part of the conspiracy has to do with the number of immigrants who will shortly be allowed into this country from Eastern Europe. The United States is about to pass immigration laws for the 1990s. These laws will multiply by at least five the number of immigrants allowed in from European nations such as East Germany, Czechoslovakia, and Hungary. With the decline of communism, people from eastern Europe are hungry for the materialism of the West.

This means America will no longer need to depend on Black males to be entry–level workers. Eastern Europeans will now become the new employable workers. They will be given these jobs as unemployment for Black men escalates. Watch the conspiracy thicken. The conspiracy is satanic. It surfaces in the economic and political and educational spheres of life, but it is all the work of the devil.

The Role of Christian Educators. Christian educators are now in the forefront of the battle. They must become the people who make the difference in turning the tide. Christian educators will do the teaching. The question is, what are they going to teach? What can one say to turn this tide?

Christian education must begin early. It must begin before four years of age. It can no longer start when people are old enough to go to Sunday School or to Training Union. It needs to start before birth. Christian educators must prepare parents to become parents. They must teach them biblical imperatives. The Christian education philosophy must start when the child is born.

This makes sense when you consider that, by the time this child reaches 18 years old, he has watched 22,000 hours of television, but he has only been in the classroom for 9,000 hours. Television educates children 2 1/2 times more than the educational system does. Television programming is full of violence, obscenity, and immorality.

If a person practiced the piano for 22,000 hours, the person would be good. If the person studied biology for 22,000 hours the person would be good. It makes sense then, that if a child watches 22,000 hours of violence, at a minimum, the child would be violent. Yet people say they don't want to bring the child to church too early. They don't want to force religion on the child. Children need to be exposed to the songs of Zion! They need to hear the worship of God's people long before they can understand it!

That is where the battle is! The brain processes 100 bytes of information a second. There are only five million bytes of information in the entire Bible. The brain can process 20 times the amount of information in the Bible every second. Imagine what the brain does in a minute, an hour, or a day.

That is why Christian education must begin with a whisper in the ear of the child, of the Word of God. We must begin by playing the Word of God on records, or cassette tapes in our homes. We must allow it to play even when we don't pay attention. In this way, it goes into their subconscious minds. It penetrates the mind, so that they will be able to use it at the appropriate time.

However, while Christians are doing this, the enemy is doing the same thing, with his music. We must fight the enemy's music by repeating God's music. Part of education is repetition. We don't always need to generate something new. Often Christian education is saying the same truth over and over again.

One of the reasons our children have the problems they have now is that parents and Christian educators have stopped repeating God's Word. Christians once took the truth of God's Word and repeated it from one generation to the next, and from one child to the next. However, we have stopped saying the things of God to our children. We have stopped singing the old songs of Zion. The old folks used to walk around the house while they were cooking, singing, "Jesus Keep Me Near the Cross" and "There Is a Fountain Filled with Blood," but we don't do that anymore. We can only fight the battle that we now face by telling this new generation about the things of God.

We don't need to use church language or religious language, because young people don't know that language. They don't know that vocabulary. However, we must raise up a new generation.

We become angry with white folks, but we can learn one thing from them. White Christians have created ways to reach their generation with the truth about Jesus Christ from the cradle to the grave. They go after their children with the Gospel very early. They form organizations like Youth for Christ, Campus Crusade, and Young Life. They take children to camp. They form the Fellowship of Christian Athletes and other such groups.

At the college level, they form groups such as Campus Crusade, Inter-Varsity Christian Fellowship, Navigators, Fellowship of Christian Athletes, and so forth. For business people and professionals, they have formed other groups. There are Executive Christian Ministries, Women Aglow, the Christian Women's Club, and the Full-Gospel Christian Businessmen and Christian Businessmen. From the cradle to the grave, white folks have the groups to reach their people. They don't extend these groups to African American communities, but they do go after their own people. I used to get angry about this, but I soon realized that they were only doing what was natural. They were reaching their generation with the Gospel. It just didn't include Blacks.

That means it is our job to reach our next generation. It is our job to save our children. It is our job to preach the Gospel to our children.

While the African American church has done remarkably well given its limited resources, it can and must do more. We must reach children through media they understand. We need to use video, rap music, and pop sound. We need to sing it, play it, sew it, picture it, draw it, wave it, and shout it everywhere! We must also support the efforts of our denominations and other groups which are trying to reach our children. The Gospel can be presented in a number of ways.

Summary. In summary, we must raise up a whole new generation of God-fearing young people who will have their minds saturated and permeated with the things of God.

Today the challenge is to educate young people about the things of God and to teach the things of God in Sunday School, Training Unions, and Christian education programs. The Bible must be the text. Also we need to start teaching reading in the church again. Sunday School may have to be the place where we use the Word of God to teach writing and how to communicate.

The challenge is to take up the mantle. We are in a desperate situation. Every time a young Black child crosses our path, we must stop and take time with him or her. Realize that the child is endangered. He may not live unless someone reaches out to him. Become surrogate fathers and mothers. Include more children in your life than your own children. It is just that desperate.

BIBLE STUDY APPLICATION

Instructions: The following exercises provide the opportunity to study 1 Corinthians 13 more closely. The first five exercises consist of short answer "discovery" questions and a summary question. The sixth exercise is an opportunity to apply principles learned from this chapter to a church-based ministry. The seventh exercise is for personal application.

> *"Though I speak with the tongues of men and of angels, and have not charity, I am become as sounding brass, or a tinkling cymbal. And though I have the gift of prophecy, and understand all mysteries, and all*

knowledge; and though I have all faith, so that I could remove mountains, and have not charity, I am nothing. And though I bestow all my goods to feed the poor, and though I give my body to be burned, and have not charity, it profiteth me nothing. Charity suffereth long, and is kind; charity envieth not; charity vaunteth not itself, is not puffed up, Doth not behave itself unseemly, seeketh not her own, is not easily provoked, thinketh no evil; Rejoiceth not in iniquity, but rejoiceth in the truth; Beareth all things, believeth all things, hopeth all things, endureth all things. Charity never faileth: but whether there be prophecies, they shall fail; whether there be tongues, they shall cease; whether there be knowledge, it shall vanish away. For we know in part, and we prophesy in part. But when that which is perfect is come, then that which is in part shall be done away. When I was a child, I spake as a child, I understood as a child, I thought as a child: but when I became a man, I put away childish things. For now we see through a glass, darkly; but then face to face: now I know in part; but then shall I know even as also I am known. And now abideth faith, hope, charity, these three; but the greatest of these is charity" (1 Corinthians 13).

1. Attempted Genocide in Bible Times

Throughout the history of the Jews, there have been several times when oppressors attempted to annihilate the entire race through an entire family line, or the males of a nation. In many instances the process began with the murdering of male children.

109

a. What circumstances surrounded the attempted elimination of males when Israel was in Egypt? (Exodus 1:1-22)

b. What circumstances surrounded Queen Athaliah's attempt to annihilate the members of an entire royal family? (2 Kings 10:12-14; 11:1-16; 2 Chronicles 22:10—23:15)

c. What circumstances surrounded the attempt to kill all Jewish males when Jews were under King Xerxes? (Esther 3)

d. During the fall of Jerusalem, why did Nebuchadnezzar remove all of the skilled Jews from Jerusalem and allow only unskilled ones to remain? (Jeremiah 52:12-16; 2 Kings 25:8-17)

e. Why might Herod have killed all of the male children? (Matthew 2:1-22)

f. SUMMARY QUESTION: What are the differences and similarities between the times when these events (a-e) took place and events taking place in the Black community today?

2. What's Love Got to Do With It?

1 Corinthians 13 says that, of the three, faith, hope and love, the greatest is love. For each of the following questions, read the two Scripture passages listed. Then, from the vantage point of a parent or youth leader, explain the role that love plays in helping young people of today.

a. 1 Corinthians 13:1; Proverbs 1:7-9

b. 1 Corinthians 13:3; Proverbs 2:1-4

c. 1 Corinthians 13:4-5; Proverbs 2:6-7

d. 1 Corinthians 13:8-10; Proverbs 4:1-5

e. 1 Corinthians 13:7; Proverbs 18:15

f. SUMMARY QUESTION: How do these passages (a-e) apply particularly to the Black male of today?

3. What's Faith Got to Do With It?

Faith is powerful. After reading each of the following passages describe the impact that faith had on relationships between youth and adults.

a. Hebrews 11:7; Genesis 6:13-7:1; 7:17-24; 8:1, 15-19; Hebrews 11:7

b. Genesis 22:1-19; Hebrews 11:17-19

c. Genesis 48:1-16; Hebrews 11:21

d. Exodus 2:1-10; Hebrews 11:23

e. John 4:46-54; Luke 7:11-15; Hebrews 11:35

f. SUMMARY QUESTION: Based on your answers to a-e, summarize the impact that faith can have on relationships between adults and troubled youth of today.

4. What's Hope Got to Do With It?

Hope, mixed with faith and love, can be powerful.

a. What is the relationship between faith and hope? (Hebrews 11:1)

b. What is the basis for hope? (1 Peter 1:3; Colossians 1:27)

c. What are some byproducts of hope in God? (Psalm 16; 22:9-11)

d. What is the hope for the future? (Romans 5:4; 1 Corinthians 13:13; 1 Peter 1:3-7, 13)

e. What brings hope to the Christian? (Romans 5:4; 1 Corinthians 13:13)

f. SUMMARY QUESTION: Based on your answers, what is the basis of the hope that we have for passing the faith to future generations?

5. Responsibilities of Women

At several points in Israel's history, the Lord raised up strong women who played important roles in the survival of their people.

a. Of what importance was Deborah's role in the survival of her people (particularly the males)? (Judges 4)

b. Of what importance was the role of Hulda in the surviva: of her people? (2 Kings 22:3-20; 23:19-28)

c. Of what importance was the role of Hoglah and her sisters in the survival of their family line? (Numbers 26:33; 27:1-11; 36:1-12; Joshua 17:3)

d. Of what significance was the role that Esther played in the survival of her people? (Esther 3:1—4:5, 12-16; 7:1—8:8; 9:1-5, 29-32)

e. Of what significance was the role that Mary Magdalene, the other Mary and the other disciples played in the survival of the human race itself? (Matthew 28:1-10; Mark 16:1-10; Luke 24:1-12)

f. SUMMARY QUESTION: Draw parallels between the roles that these women played and those that various African American women play today. At times when the men and women of their communities would have been "endangered species," how have these women helped? Based on these passages, should Black women abandon involvement with the plight of Black males? Explain your answer.

6. CHURCH–BASED MINISTRY

Based on your answers to exercises 1-5, design (or improve) a program for your local church. The programs should involve training adults to help the "endangered species." Be sure to include, in your design, roles that African American women can play.

7. PERSONAL APPLICATION

In your daily life, what contact do you have with the "endangered species"? How can you become personally involved in helping our young men and women to survive?

CHAPTER SIX

Aisha, 14, stood at the front of the church, facing the congregation and swaying back and forth as the choir marched in. "We're marching, marching up to Zion." As they sang, Aisha was careful to catch every word, as she "signed" for the five deaf brothers and sisters sitting on the front pew.

Aisha and her family had just recently arrived to Chicago from Mississippi. At first people were not that friendly to her. Then her family joined Pilgrim Baptist Church. She accepted Christ as her personal Saviour, and Brother Hasberry of the New Life Ministry told her about some classes where people were being trained to "sign" for the deaf.

Aisha was so happy that she had learned this new skill. Now she really felt a part of this exciting church. She wasn't a foreigner anymore. She was a part of God's family. Now she could use her gifts to help others grow in the Lord.

Throughout history, the African American church has played a powerful role in the lives of African American youth. The story of Aisha is one among many examples. However, today Black church youth are confronted with serious challenges brought on by special problems which so many African American youth must face.

Current statistics reflect both positive and negative realities. On the positive side, the American Council on Education reports that the gap between Black and white youth who graduate from high school is narrowing. Today 76.1% of Black youth graduate compared to 82.1% for whites, and 30.8% of Black youth attend college compared to 38.8% for white youth.[1]

On the negative side, the U.S. Census Bureau reports that only 37% of Black children are born into two–parent families, compared to 77% of white youth.[2] The U.S. Department of Commerce reports that 43.2% of Black families with children who are 18 or under are in poverty, compared to 14.1% for white families.[3] The U.S. Department of Labor reports that the unemployment rate for Black youth is 12.2%, compared to 5.3% for white youth.[4] The National Center for Health Statistics reports that 48% of Black males who die between the ages of 15-19, die of gunshot wounds, compared to 18% for white youth.[5]

A recent Gallup Poll reported that 54% of Black youth who were interviewed felt that drug abuse was the biggest problem facing young people.[6]

In response to these realities, Black churches are reaching out to young people in a variety of ways. However, research indicates a need for a wider range of strategies to reach today's youth. Lincoln and Mamiya interviewed 2,150 church representatives and found that while 20% had activities such as rallies, youth choruses and scout groups, only 11.4% had educational programs specifically targeted at youth, and less than 10% had recreational programs, counseling, scholarships or special youth ministers.[7]

Is it possible that if Black churches had a better range of services for youth, they might help youth meet more of the challenges they now face?

In the following article, Dr. Bennie Goodwin addresses three critical questions that must be answered by local Black churches if the Black church and Black youth are to survive and make an impact on the African American community.

PREPARING THE NEXT GENERATION

Dr. Bennie E. Goodwin
Isaiah 6:1-5

Youth Are Important. Young people are one of our most important resources. They represent both our past and future. They come to us as gifts from God, innocent and unspoiled. We make them what they become, and can rejoice in or lament over our handiwork.

They have potential for both good and evil. They can become Hitlers or Gandhis, Jezebels or Florence Nightingales, Delilahs or Mary Bethunes, Al Capones or Martin Luther Kings. To a great extent, what they become depends on what we are and what we do to them, for them and with them![8]

In this chapter we want to ask and answer three questions: 1) Who are our youth? 2) How can the church help youth survive? and 3) How can youth help the church survive?

Who Are Our Youth? There is a distinction between "youth" and "young people." The phrase "young people" refers to persons up to 34 years of age.

"Youth," on the other hand, is a technical term and refers to persons between the ages of 12-17. These persons are normally in junior and senior high school and are also referred to as "teens" or "teenagers." The chart that follows shows how they fit into the total age range.

Birth-11—children
12-17—youth
18-34—young adulthood
35-64—middle adulthood
65 and over—later adulthood[9]

Keep in mind, when we say youth, we're talking about young people between the ages of 12 and 17.

Who are youth? They are young people between the ages of 12 and 17. Physically they are energetic and changing. Mentally they are optimistic and skeptical. Socially they run in groups and spiritually they are open and seeking. Their interests are many and center primarily around themselves as they seek to explore life and enjoy it. Their problems seem usually to stem from negative peer pressure and their needs are generally for academic achievement and spiritual commitment. Their potential is unknown and practically unlimited—for either good or evil. They are our greatest challenges. They can raise us to unbounded joy or plunge us into deepest sorrow.

Humanly speaking, our longterm future is in their hands. By their decisions and actions we will survive or perish.

How Can the Church Help Youth Survive? *The Situation.* What is the situation with our youth, particularly in the Black community? The situation is that many of our youth are in trouble. They are in trouble because of 1) poor preparation at home, 2) inadequate education at school, 3) negative peer pressure in the community and 4) a lack of positive impact by the church. As a result of these liabilities, we have high rates of abuse at home, high dropout rates at school, crime, gang wars, and substance abuse in our streets, low youth attendance and participation in our churches and an 80% Black male population in our prisons.

What the Church Can Do. The situation is so tragic that we must ask for and accept help from any and all available sour-

116

ces—business, government, social and civic organizations—anywhere. But let's concentrate on what the church can do, and in some cases is already doing.

Reach, Teach and Equip. Before the church can contribute anything lasting to the survival of our youth, it must reach them. Many young people have already given up on the church, but the church must not give up on them. Wherever our youth are, that's where effective ministries go! There are churches and church–related ministries that are making a positive difference in young people's lives. They go where the youth are.

They go into the streets (that's where Dave Wilkerson met and introduced Nicky Cruz to Jesus Christ).[10] They go into the schools (yes, there are ways of getting into the schools). They go into the youth detention centers and jails. (Malcolm X was converted to the Black Muslim religion while in a Boston jail).[11] They go on T.V. and radio (Tom Skinner was saved while listening to a gospel radio program).[12]

Serious youth ministry reaches out to young people wherever they are—in the streets, schools and prisons—and by whatever means they can use—tracts, radio, television, sports, camps and conferences.

They reach youth for Christ and the church. It is not enough just to make contact with young people. If they are to survive the forces of evil in our neighborhood and the larger society, they need a change from the inside out. They need a spiritual change. They need a new life, the strength of character, the joy and hope that Jesus Christ offers. They need to be saved (Acts 16:30-1), forgiven (1 John 1:9), born again (John 3:7), delivered, and changed (2 Corinthians 5:17). And even with this inward spiritual experience, it's going to be rough and difficult to survive. But without a spiritual change, it is virtually impossible.

We must reach youth with the Good News of God's love and power. He loves them just as they are—no matter who they are or how they are. But He also has the power to change them and that's good news too!

The churches that have effective youth ministries do more than reach young people with the message of Christ's love and power. They draw them into a church. And the churches with dynamic, thriving ministries do at least four things:[13]

1. They involve their youth in serious but joyful Christian worship.
2. They involve them in well-planned and relevant Christian education ministries.
3. They involve them in a variety of Christian recreation and fellowship activities.
4. They involve them in various short– and long term Christian service projects that are interesting and helpful.

In summary, they reach youth with the Gospel message of Jesus Christ, they teach them for spiritual, mental, emotional and social growth, and they equip them for Christian service.

Prepare Them. There is a final thing these effective churches do—they help prepare youth for life in a pluralistic society that is dominated by white folk. Now this subject requires a book by itself.[14] But let's look at four ways these churches seek to achieve this purpose:

1. They instill in their youth a consciousness of their African American identity.
2. They instill in their youth a love and respect for Black folk.
3. They instill in their youth an awareness of the identity and nature of their oppressors.
4. They impress upon their youth the priority of serving the African American community.

These purposes are achieved through the study of African American history and contemporary culture, through exposure to persons of outstanding achievement, through travel to libraries and museums, colleges and universities, churches and conferences, as well as concerts and art exhibits where the achievements of African American people are displayed and celebrated.

118

Youth are also prepared for leadership through participation in organizations such as the National Association for the Advancement of Colored People (NAACP), Southern Christian Leadership Conference (SCLC), the Urban League, People United to Save Humanity (PUSH), Opportunity Industrial Centers (OIC), and other organizations on the local, state and national level that plan, protest, pressure and push for equal opportunities for African Americans and other oppressed people.

Do these kinds of youth ministries bear fruit? Yes, they do. It is such ministries that gave us the Christian leaders of the civil rights movement—the Andrew Youngs, the Ralph Abernathys, the Jesse Jacksons, the Rosa Parks, the Martin Luther King, Sr.'s and Jr.'s, the Coretta Kings and many more. These persons didn't appear at random. The Black church helped them survive and prepared them to lead in the 50s, 60s, 70s and 80s. Now it is our challenge to prepare leadership for the 21st century. Our youth can and will survive as they are reached, taught and prepared for leadership by the Black Church.

How Youth Can Help the Church Survive. Three key institutions are responsible for the survival of African Americans in the United States: the African American church, schools and extended family. Of these three the Black Church has been the most crucial. It is therefore of utmost importance that the Black Church survive. The question we want to explore in this section is: How can youth aid in the church's survival? I believe there are at least five ways that they may do so: 1) by becoming consistent, longterm church members, 2) by being enthusiastic church advocates, 3) by being church supporters by their presence, participation and giving, 4) by serving as church leaders and 5) by serving the African American community as model Christians and citizens. Let's look briefly at each of these suggestions.

As Church Members. Our youth are the saplings from which the trees of tomorrow's forest will grow. Without them the church will be a barren, desolate wasteland. The doors of our churches will be locked and the windows boarded up. The pews will be empty and the choir and pulpit silent. Where then will Black folk go for encouragement and spiritual uplift? Where will they gather to sing and shout? Where will they receive the bread of life and the refreshing water of the Spirit?

Today's effective churches are welcoming youth into their membership. They are making places for them on the pews and in their Christian education ministry. They are asking their youth to serve as junior deacons, ushers, and stewards as well as to continue to be a part of the traditional junior choir and music ministry. In churches that intend to survive, youth are included as a part of the church's district, state, national and international programs.

As Church Advocates. During the 1960s a popular outdoor sport was to stand on the corner and "run down" the church. And of course, some of the criticism was justified. The church has never been perfect; after all it's made up of imperfect human beings. But in spite of all of the "put downs" of the church on the corner, on radio and television, on the stage and in the movies, in cartoons and comic books, it is without dispute the most effective institution that we have.

The Black church is the birthplace of most of our lasting community institutions, including many of our Black colleges, insurance companies, financial institutions and civil rights organizations. And whoever heard of a Black politician getting elected without stopping by the church? If we can inform our young people of where Thurgood Marshall, Mary Bethune, Medgar Evers, Whitney Houston, John Johnson, Oprah Winfrey and Lou Rawls have their roots, then perhaps when they pass by street corners where our churches are being ridiculed, they can say something positive to set the record straight and give a balanced perspective to a sometimes unjustified criticism of the Black Church.

As Church Supporters. During our last five years in Atlanta, I was Christian Education Director of a large church with an effective ministry to the community. But I was surprised to know how many of the 4,000 or so members attended church spasmodically, participated in the on-going program of the church minimally and gave $1.00 in church when they did attend. One Sunday morning the pastor told this story about a conversation between some dollar bills:

One Dollar Bill: *Man, where have you been? I haven't seen you around lately.*

Ten Dollar Bill: *I've been to London and Israel and visited Ghana before I returned to the States. Where have you been?*

One Dollar Bill: *Man, I haven't been nowhere. Seems like I've spent my whole life in church!*

How can we convince our youth that the church is not like Grandmother's house, where you visit only on holidays, nor is it like a football game, where you go to be entertained but not to participate. We can make a strong impression on them with good, sound Bible teaching, honest record keeping, strict accountability (doing with the money what we said we were going to do), and by being a good example. If we can do these things, I believe we can then challenge the youth to follow us. And by their consistent presence, participation and financial support, we can insure the church's survival.

As Church Leaders. At the beginning of a Youth Day sermon entitled "You Can Make a Difference," I asked the young people this question: What do these people have in common: Frederick Douglass, Sojourner Truth, Charles Harrison Mason, Madame C.J. Walker and Martin Luther King, Jr.? They gave three answers: 1) they were all Black. 2) they all made a difference. 3) they are all dead!

At the end of each year we look back and count our casualities. Who is going to take the places of our outstanding leaders? Our youth! If not them, who? Who will lead our churches and communities? The Hispanics? The American Indians? The Asians? No, we must lead our own communities. Let's then prepare our youth and challenge them to lead our churches in helping meet the critical needs of our churches and communities.

As Community Leaders. Historically most of our outstanding Black leaders have either been church leaders or have had their roots in the Black church. Effective leadership is usually the result of training, opportunity and experience. For African Americans, the church is where these three components come together most easily.[15]

Without exploring the historical and theological basis for this assertion, let's just say that if our church is to produce effective community leaders, we must give our youth training, opportunity and experience. And we must encourage them to actively participate in the life and leadership of the community as model Christians and good citizens.

Model Christians. Jesus' disciples were probably flabbergasted when He told them that they were the light of the world and that they were to let their lights shine so the world could see (Matthew 5:14-16). I'm sure they wondered how this could possibly be true. They were aware that they were just a rather unorganized, uneducated, unsophisticated group of country youth. It took them a while, but once they received spiritual insight and power, they not only survived but laid the foundation for the transformation of the Roman Empire.

If by our teaching and example we can motivate our youth to live the Christian life at home, at school, at work and play; then to teach them to take the next step of being good citizens will be challenging but not impossible.

Good Citizens. It is important to register and vote, to write our legislators and to keep informed about the major issues. It is important to participate in the PTA, to support our unions, to give to the Red Cross and the American Cancer Fund. It is important to be a member of the NAACP and to take part in community planning and protests. It is important to know what's happening in Africa and to encourage our church leadership, laity larity and youth to go to the motherland to see firsthand the beauty and tragedy of our homeland. Granted, very few people can do all these things effectively. But if each of us works in the area of his or her special interest and encourages others to work in theirs, not only will our youth survive and the church survive but the world will survive a little longer as well.

> To each is given a bag of tools
> A shapeless mass, a book of rules
> And each must make e'er life has flow
> And stumbling block or stepping stone.

BIBLE STUDY APPLICATION

Instructions: The following exercises provide the opportunity to study more closely the points that Dr. Goodwin raises in his essay. The first five exercises consist of short answer "discovery" questions and a summary question. The sixth exercise is an opportunity to apply principles learned from this chapter to a church-based ministry. The seventh exercise is for personal application.

> *"In the year that king Uzziah died I saw also the Lord sitting upon a throne, high and lifted up, and his train filled the temple. Above it stood the seraphims: each one had six wings; with twain he covered his face, and with twain he covered his feet, and with twain he did fly. And one cried unto another, and said, Holy, holy, holy, is the Lord of hosts: the whole earth is full of his glory. And the posts of the door moved at the voice of him that cried, and the house was filled with smoke. Then said I, Woe is me! for I am undone; because I am a man of unclean lips, and I dwell in the midst of a people of unclean lips: for mine eyes have seen the King, the Lord of hosts" (Isaiah: 6:1-5).*

1. Hagar and Ishmael

Hagar raised a son under very difficult circumstances.

a. Describe the circumstances surrounding Ishmael's birth. (Genesis 16:1-4, 15)

b. In what type of emotional climate was Ishmael born, and how might this have affected his personality? (Genesis 16:1-5)

c. In what type of emotional climate did Ishmael spend his formative years, and how might this have affected him? (Genesis 21:1-16)

d. Who and what were responsible for the survival of Hagar and Ishmael? (Genesis 21:17-19)

e. Fill in the "words between the lines" that might account for Hagar's success in raising her son. (Genesis 21:20-21)

f. SUMMARY QUESTION: Dr. Goodwin, in his introduction, asks how the church can help young people survive. Does Hagar's experience provide any clues? How might youth leaders, parents and pastors learn from her experience? What parallels might there be between the experiences of Hagar and Isaiah in this chapter's Scripture passage?

2. Moses and Joshua

The older man Moses was the mentor of the young Joshua.

a. In what type of family environment did Joshua live and how might this have provided training for him? (Numbers 13:16; 1 Chronicles 7:20-25; Numbers 1:1-16; 2:1-2, 18-24; 7:1-3, 12-83; 10:11-12, 22)

b. Who were Joshua's mentors within the Community of Faith? (Exodus 17:8-11; 24:12-14; 33:7-11; Numbers 11:24-29; Deuteronomy 1:34-38)

c. As a result of his training, what services did Joshua provide in the Community of Faith? (Numbers 13:1-17; 14:1-9; Exodus 17:8-16; Deuteronomy 1:38; 3:28; 31:14, 23; 34:9)

d. Who took the mantle of leadership after Moses? How was this possible? (Numbers 27:18-23; 32:28-30; 24:16-28; Deuteronomy 3:21-28, 14-15, 23; 34:9)

e. Dr. Goodwin asks how the church can help youth to help the church survive. How did the Community of Faith help Joshua to help Israel survive? (Numbers 27:63-65; 32:10-15)

f. SUMMARY QUESTION: Consider the role that the family and the Faith Community played in Joshua's life. Are there any insights that can be gleaned from this story concerning the role that the family and the church can play in the lives of young people today?

3. Deborah and Barak

Deborah, a woman in the Faith Community, helped to make Barak into a warrior.

a. Barak was from Kedesh. What type of historical significance did the Israelites attach to Kedesh? (Number 14:4; Genesis 16:7, 14; 20:4; Numbers 20:1, 2-11, 14-21; Deuteronomy 2:1)

b. Who was Deborah? (Judges 4:4-5)

c. When Deborah summoned Barak, what type of challenge was she asking him to face? (Judges 4:2-3, 6-7)

d. How was Barak enabled to meet this challenge? (Judges 4:8-10, 14)

e. What was the outcome of Deborah's work with Barak? (Judges 4:15-16; 5:1-30)

f. SUMMARY QUESTION: In many situations in the African American community today, there is a shortage of African American men. This is obvious in families, churches and schools. Young Black men need to be developed into leaders. Does the story of Deborah and Barak provide any insight for Black women finding themselves in the situation of raising, teaching and mentoring today?

4. Saul and Jonathan

In some ways, Saul was a good father. In others, he was a very poor model for his son.

a. Describe the family life of Saul, Jonathan's father. (1 Samuel 9:1-8; 1 Chronicles 8:33-34; Judges 5:11-14) How might this have influenced the environment in which Jonathan grew up?

b. Summarize some events from the history of the tribe of Benjamin (Saul and Jonathan's tribe). How might Saul have influenced Jonathan? (Judges 19—21)

c. What environment surrounded the immediate family of Saul and Jonathan? (1 Samuel 14:49-52) How might this environment have affected Jonathan? (1 Samuel 13:2, 3; 14:1, 4-23; 20:1-9)

d. Saul was very insecure. What might have caused him to be so insecure? (1 Samuel 9:25—10:1, 20-22; 18:5-11; 2:1-18, 22-26; 3:20; 4:17-18; 8:5-10; 9:15-17)

e. How did Saul's insecurity affect the way he raised Jonathan? (1 Samuel 14:24-45; 19:1-6; 20:25-33; 29:1—31:1)

f. SUMMARY QUESTION: Today some African American families are wealthier than African American families have ever been. However, these same families are surrounded by a Black community that is largely impoverished. Moreover, certain realities in the economy could plunge working and middle income families into poverty at any time. To what extent are such families similar and different from Saul's family? In this type of uncertain environment, are there any mistakes that parents typically make? In what ways are they similar and different from mistakes that Saul made?

5. David and Absalom

In many ways, David was an excellent role model for his children. He was in a position to demonstrate to them how to follow the Lord. However, in his relationships with women, he set a very poor example.

a. How many different wives and children did David have? (1 Samuel 27:3; 2 Samuel 2—3; 5:15-16; 1 Chronicles 3:1-5; 14:4-5)

b. What were some of David's other involvements with women? (2 Samuel 11:1—13:29)

c. What evidence is there that David may have transmitted the wrong attitudes about sex, women and murder to his children? (2 Samuel 13:1, 6, 10-11, 14, 20, 23, 28-29, 37, 39)

d. Which child was Absalom, son of David, and what was his particular background? (2 Samuel 3:2-3)

e. How did Absalom become a problem for David and the entire community? (2 Samuel 13:23-29, 37, 38, 39; 14; 15:1—16:23; 17:1-14, 21-24; 19:10; 17:25, 26; 18:1-18)

f. SUMMARY QUESTION: Since the "sexual revolution" of the 1970s, American society in general, along with many Christian leaders, has relaxed former standards regarding sexual morality. Parents, preachers, youth leaders, and other adults are often heard telling young people to "Do as I say, not as I do." Is it possible for young people to do this? What lessons can be learned from David's relationship with Absalom?

6. CHURCH–BASED MINISTRY

Suppose that your church is interested in offering a series of parenting seminars. Considering your answers to these exercises, what are some possible weekly topics for a 10-week series?

7. PERSONAL APPLICATION

In some aspect of your life, you no doubt have a contact or a relationship with African American young people. You may be a parent, youth leader, uncle, aunt, cousin, neighbor, teacher, social worker, doctor, school secretary, or Sunday School teacher. Write at least one goal that you can set for helping this endangered generation to survive. Then write another goal for how you can help a representative of this younger generation to help the Black church and the Black community to survive.

CHAPTER SEVEN

Some men and women could be seen slowly gathering in the church library for the monthly executive council meeting. Today, Vanessa Carter, the new DCE, would present a proposal to organize a new Board of Christian Education. Mrs. Lewis, Mrs. Lipscomb, Mrs. Locke, Mr. Kennilworth and Mr. Brown could be seen whispering in the corner.

"We've already got one council, why do we need another one?" Mr. Brown asked. "What are they trying to do? Get rid of our council and put in another one? I could have stayed home if I knew that somebody was gonna be telling me what I haven't been doing for the past fifty years."

"Who does she think she is anyway?" Mrs. Lewis continued. "How come the pastor lets her come in and take over? Me and my family had to work our way in, pay our dues. Then we could say how something ought to be done. Where's she from anyway? Her family doesn't belong to this church."

Mr. Brown interrupted, "Anyway, the pastor is the director of Christian education. He's the one that runs things. What's she trying to do? Steal his pulpit?"

"These little light-skinned proper-talkin' girls always get what they want," continued Mrs. Locke, a large, dark-skinned elderly woman. "They get a little

education and come in trying to make Black people act like white people do."

"Yeah, you see, there is a basic point that these so-called educated people don't understand," said Mr. Kennilworth. "The Black church is an organism—not an organization. God never meant for things to get too organized. Bringing all of this newfangled stuff into the church is wrong."

"We don't need no training. All we need is the Holy Ghost and a little mother wit." Mrs. Lewis laughed. "That's what's made the church what it is—not no Boards of Christian Education and DECs, DCEs or whatever."

"She's out of her place, if you ask me," Mrs. Lipscomb butted in. "The Bible says that women are not supposed to take leadership in the church. The only place for a woman is in the church kitchen with the rest of us."

"She acts like she's trying to be important, if you ask me," Mrs. Lewis added. "Just 'cause she's got a degree she feels she is better than other women."

"The basic problem is that the Black church wasn't meant to be a business or a school. It was meant for worship and having a good time. Why can't she see that? Where's she been all her life?" Mr. Kennilworth laughed. "She's gonna be in for a surprise."

"That's her problem, not mine!" Mrs. Locke said. "There's plenty for a young person her age to do around here, like singing in the choir or ushering. She needs to learn to respect her elders."

"All she talks about is that Black stuff," Mr. Kennilworth said. "God is not Black, and He's not white. He's a universal God. You know, she's just like the pastor with his politics. If you ask me, both of them are militants."

"And why are they always talking about giving away stuff? A lot of the people they talk about helping don't want no help," added Mrs. Lewis.

"You're right! The Bible says that if you take one step, God will take two. The trouble with a lot of the people they're trying to help is that they don't want to help themselves," Mr. Brown added, just as the chairperson of the executive council called the meeting to order.

A number of controversial issues are expressed in the opening conversations. One is the issue of African American professionals and the use of their expertise in the Black church. Then there is the issue of whether women (other than ministers) should be allowed to assume professional but nontraditional leadership roles in the church. Another issue is whether the church should involve itself with the needs of poor people, and then there is the issue of whether young people should assume leadership roles in the church, outside of ushering and singing in the choir.

Lincoln and Mamiya conducted a random nationwide survey of Black churches. They found that, of paid church staff members listed, the most common titles were pastor, secretary, custodian and musician. Professional directors of Christian education and other professionals were not among those com-

*monly listed. In the same population of interviewees, only 5.3%
reported cooperating with community social agencies related to
solutions of problems in any of the following areas: employment
(5.3%), drug and alcohol agencies and programs (4.4%), senior
citizen programs (7.6%), welfare rights and housing problems
(7.3%), food and clothing programs (6.8%), tutoring and educational programs (5.2%), and youth agencies (18.8%).[1]*

*Youth groups were active in 82.6% of the 2,150 churches in-
terviewed. However, in terms of Sunday School membership, out
of a total average attendance of 390 per Sunday School representative interviewed, there was an average number of only 58
youth per Sunday School. Moreover, the highest percentage of
church programs for youth were in the areas of youth choirs,
youth groups or scout groups, and the percentage of churches
having these programs was only 20.1%.[2]*

*When asked why they feel youth leave the church, 48.6%
(nearly half) of the church representatives felt that, either youth
were not given a chance to participate meaningfully, there was a
lack of programs relevant for youth, or there was a lack of intellectual challenges for youth.[3]*

*Dr. Colleen Birchett, in the following article, discusses con-
troversies surrounding each of the following groups: African
American professionals, Black women as leaders, Black youth,
and the "Have Nots." She also discusses why each of these
groups is essential for the survival of the church into the 21st
century.*

CHURCH CONFLICTS

Dr. Colleen Birchett
1 Samuel 4:1-3, 5-11, 14-18

The scene in the above Scripture opens with the Children of Israel in battle with the Philistines. For the time being, the Philistines have defeated the Israelites. As they glanced around at the devastation, no doubt their sense of despair was not unlike that which is felt by many African Americans today, viewing the devastation that has swept through so many African American communities.

However, it is noteworthy that immediately following their defeat, the Israelites turned to God. Immediately, they sent for the Ark of the Covenant, the symbol of God's presence among them. At the renewed sight of the Ark of the Covenant the people shouted for joy. One can almost hear the sounds swelling up from the pages of 1 Samuel 4. It reminds one of a good old-fashioned Black church revival held in the heat of summer. It was just this type of old-fashioned revival that frightened the Philistines (4:6-10).

That same type of old-fashioned revival frightened American slavemasters during slavery. Like the Philistines, the slavemasters realized that the worship experience itself could stimulate unity and empowerment among God's people. It is no wonder that slavemasters made it illegal for Black people to hold church services.

However, it is important to remember that at the time of the battle between the Israelites and the Philistines, the leaders of Israel—Eli's two sons—had turned away from the Lord (1 Samuel 2:12-17), and their behavior had caused disunity and a spiritual decline among the people (3:11-14).

It is no wonder that the Philistines could overcome the Israelites before they could fully unify for battle. The Philistines captured the Ark of the Covenant and killed the Israelite leaders (4:11). When Eli heard that the Ark of the Covenant had been removed from among God's people, he fell over and died. He realized that the removal of this symbol symbolized the absence of God, and signalled a death knell for community spirit.

Today, the African American church in the African American community has a role that is similar to that which the Ark of the Covenant had in Israel. It symbolizes the presence of God in that community.

However, just as the Ark of the Covenant was endangered at the time of the battle with the Philistines, many Black churches are endangered today. As in the days of Eli's sons, disunity exists among the leadership and among the people. Endangered Black churches are now placed at risk both by pressures from outside and pressures from within.

The pressures from within many churches are caused by tensions between various elements over issues related to change. The changes that are in dispute usually have to do with how to integrate new people and new ideas; that is, how to practice 1 Corinthians 12.

On one side are those who want either to strictly regulate the rate at which new people, ideas, programs and roles become an accepted part of the church, or chase them out. On the other side are those who represent these new forces and are finding it difficult to gain acceptance and the integration of their gifts. Very closely related to this conflict are issues of how or whether to pass the mantle of church leadership to the next generation.

This is a critical issue for Black churches at the end of the 20th century, because the generation currently in power within the church must decide whether to pass on the mantle, or allow their individual church to die with them and their generation.

Churches and church programs must be modernized if they are to survive beyond the current century. Sadly, though, people who are most equipped to bring about this modernization are most frequently isolated and rejected.

Full–scale war can erupt over this issue, with the pastor in the middle, facing the threat of a split church. However, this internal conflict over change must be resolved. This chapter focuses on conflict related to issues of change. It is based on information that we have gathered as the Association of Black Directors of Christian Education of which I serve as president. In our interviews with Directors of Christian Education from around the country, the following patterns emerge.

There appear to be four centers of resistance to change. First there is the struggle between those who are aging and those who are young. Then there is a struggle between Black men and Black women. A third struggle is between those who are formally trained or educated and those who do not have formal training, and a fourth struggle is between the "haves" and the "have nots." Let's first examine the struggle between the ages.

The Struggle Between the Generations. In many churches, young people are not allowed to participate on any other level than ushering and singing in the choir. Moreover, the very attitudes of older people suggest that the lives of young people are not taken seriously. One evidence of this is when examples from lives of the young are not used to illustrate spiritual principles. Instead, memorizing is emphasized, and personal applications are de-emphasized. Older people often complain that young people talk too much. Many expect youth to speak only when they are addressed. They often feel that talking with a young person would not retain the older person in a superior position.

The struggle is on both sides of the generation gap. Nevertheless people of both age groups need to listen to each other in order for the mantle of leadership to be passed to the next generation.

Another form of this conflict is the resistance on the part of older people to allow modern Christian music into the church. Older people often reject any variety in church music. They insist on Christian music that only represents their generation. However, rejecting modern Christian music which appeals to youth really involves rejecting youth themselves. At least many young people feel rejected because of this.

Another evidence of this conflict is what often occurs on Youth Sunday in many churches. In many churches, large numbers of adults stay at home on Youth Sunday. This says to young people that they are of less importance than adults. Some people even walk out when a young person begins to deliver a speech. They don't do this when the pastor is talking, but when one of the children is talking, they head for the restroom. That is another negative gesture to young people, and it is a sign of resistance against integrating young people into the church.

Part of the challenge of dealing with the conflict of the ages is that African Americans are dealing within the framework of a Eurocentric attitude toward aging. In Eurocentric culture, aged people are often put "on a shelf," so to speak. However, pushing older people aside is not consistent with the traditional African centered view of aging. In Africa older people and younger people co-exist in the village. Both older people and younger people have very vital roles in the community. No one is put "on a shelf" or in an "old folks' home."

Faced with the Eurocentric culture, many older people fear that younger people will push them aside and then out of church. Hence the older generation tends to resist change.

It may be that this resistance can be overcome if young people make a conscious effort to see that the founders and builders of their churches do not feel that they are being pushed out. The Black Church must do everything in its power to enlist both new and old gifts in the building of the church for the 21st century.

The Struggle Between the Sexes. Let's now focus on the conflict between males and females. Again, we must consider that this conflict is taking place within a Eurocentric culture that has manipulated it. It is difficult to examine this conflict without considering the background of slavery which led to the distorted concepts that Black men and women often have of one another. We must also examine it in the context of more recent developments in the age of affirmative action, when white male researchers and sociologists delivered the lie that the problem of the Black man was the Black woman, not the white man.

Let's first examine slavery. During slavery, Black women were defined as breeders and workhorses. If a Black woman stepped outside of that role, she was often punished or killed. Black men were considered studs and workhorses. Both men and women were considered 3/5 of a person. There was no other definition. Both were chattel slaves.

One of the results of slavery is that many Black women and men accepted images of themselves and one another from their oppressors. Therefore they see themselves primarily in sexual or servile terms. While motherhood is certainly one of the most beautiful experiences in the world, it is not the only role that a Black woman is capable of performing. Neither is sexual intercourse. Neither is house cleaning. There is no reason that a Black woman should feel that she is out of her place unless she restricts herself to jobs involving physical labor—back-breaking jobs—that do not require the use of the intellect. There is also no reason for her to pressure fellow Black women into remaining in such a caste with her, even if she chooses to think of herself only in those terms.

Women are often their own worst enemies in this respect. Moreover, this conflict among women is often exploited and manipulated by Black and white men who are afraid to allow women to have power, based on education and training. Many men are afraid that, if such women have power, the women will do something evil to them, or take away their power.

At a minimum, they often feel that the woman may "show them up." Often there is much more fear about being "shown up" by a Black woman than of being "shown up" by a Black man. Threatened Black men and threatened Black women sometimes form alliances to frustrate the achievements of educated and trained Black women.

However, all Black men are not like this. There are other types of Black men. There are those who, rather than frustrate Black women, encourage them and benefit from their talents. African American men who have known how to capitalize on the skills of Black women have emerged as successful. Their churches are larger and, even if small, more effective. Reverend Jesse Jackson and Mayor Harold Washington are examples of people who have capitalized on the skills of Black women in other spheres, incorporating them at every level of their operations.

If the Black church is going to be equipped for the 21st century, it cannot eliminate the intellectual capabilities of more than half of its members. In many churches, the percentage would be closer to 90%.

As mentioned before, another source of this conflict is a result of misinformation which has come to Black men from white conservative sociologists who claim that educated Black women are taking jobs from Black men. This is one of the arguments used against affirmative action programs. However, no one has presented any statistics to prove that Black women are the real culprits in keeping Black men out of jobs. Neither has anyone produced a logical argument that Black men would get more jobs if Black women restricted themselves to day work (house cleaning).

One of the results of the irrational fears associated with this conflict is that highly trained Black women (particularly at the Ph.D. level) are frustrated when they attempt to use their skills within the auxiliaries and ministries of the church. One of the most common arenas of this type of warfare is in Christian Education programs where public school educators attempt to refine the means by which the "old old story" is passed on to youth. It also occurs when such women attempt to refine outreach programs, and it almost always occurs when women try to provide input in any area considered reserved for men only.

Many women who do not have formal training are very jealous and threatened by women who are formally trained— particularly if the woman in question is younger than they are. Many such women, rather than take the initiative to acquire training themselves, find it easier to use their intelligence to creatively sabotage the leadership of trained women. Many don't see anything wrong with it. They feel that this is what they are expected to do.

In interviewing trained women who have become victims of such sabotage efforts, a pattern emerges. In this pattern, the untrained women sometimes form coalitions with men (both trained and untrained) and sometimes work against the success of programs initiated or designed by trained women. If this is brought to the attention of the pastor, to cover up what is happening, these coalitions sometimes may allow one or two trained Black women into them. That is, as long as these one or two "tokens" help them keep most trained Black women out of leadership. It is a pattern that is very similar to strategies that white people in white corporate America have used to control the number of Blacks who climb the corporate ladder.

These coalitions form easily because it is still true that only a minority of Black women have gone far enough in school to achieve formal degrees and professional training. It is difficult for the average person to realize that a pattern is occurring across the country because, in most small congregations, there are less than five formally trained Black women. However, if a person could take a global or more panoramic view of the relationships between Black women and Black men in churches, the person would see the pattern very clearly. This is often the case with trained Black women who assume the role of Director of Christian Education.

However, this "status quo" concerning the suppression of women's leadership could not be maintained if the majority of women did not cooperate with it. If the "status quo" were changed, all women would benefit from it—not just formally trained women.

Often the Black men involved in the resistance, use logic based on information and biblical interpretations from certain white religious conservatives many of whose ancestors used the same logic related to Blacks to make it illegal for Black people to improve themselves or their institutions. Like slavemasters and Philistines of old, these people of recent times know what it

139

would mean for Black women to be given the freedom to help develop the Black church.

These "Philistines" are pushing an alternative religion of self-worship which makes the satisfaction of the male ego more important than the survival of the Black Church into the 21st century. If, like the Sons of Eli, Black men buy into this way of thinking, it will be to the detriment of the entire race.

The Struggle Involving Professionals. Traditionally many Black professionals have not felt welcome to use their gifts in the church. While most are employed in professions that build the white man's institutions, they are often not allowed to use their skills to build their own institutions. For example, sometimes professional accountants are not allowed anywhere near church finances. However, the services of trained lawyers and accountants will be needed in the future if the church is to be strong enough to resist financial pressures. The church must ask itself why it sends young people away to school and tells them to give back to the Black community, yet when they return, it rejects them and tells them to "stay in their place."

The Struggle Between the Haves and the Have Nots. Let's now examine the conflict between the haves and the have nots. While churches may be uneasy with Black professionals, churches are often even less comfortable with people who are at the bottom of the economic spectrum. These are not the Ph.D.'s, but the A.D.C.s!

Some churches will showcase high-achieving people who hold important positions in the community as long as they don't get too involved with the church's internal affairs. However, some members of the same church "frown" on people who live in housing projects and cannot afford the best of clothing. In some churches, one has to have a high political profile in the community in order to become a deacon—even though the Bible has an entirely different requirement for being a deacon. That is why many people who do not fit a "high class" profile do not feel welcome in certain churches.

In order to change attitudes and create a church that is more open to "Have nots," it is important to consider the ministry of our Lord Jesus Christ, who did not confine Himself to the Jewish synagogue, debating with the elite Pharisees and Sadducees. He walked along the hillsides and valleys, ministering to the sick and emotionally ill. He has told us to do likewise (Matthew 28:17-20).

Summary. In order for the African American Church to equip itself to carry out its mission, it must deal with these basic conflicts over the issues of change. In each of these categories, Christian education programs must teach solutions for resolving conflicts between the above-mentioned elements, with the goal of co-existence in mind.

BIBLE STUDY APPLICATION

Instructions: The following exercises provide the opportunity to take a closer look at 1 Samuel 4:1-18, and at some issues currently dividing our churches. The first five exercises consist of short answer, discovery questions and a summary question. The sixth exercise provides the opportunity to make applications of knowledge gained to a church-based ministry. The seventh question allows for personal application.

"And the word of Samuel came to all Israel. Now Israel went out against the Philistines to battle, and pitched beside Eben-ezer: and the Philistines pitched in Aphek. And the Philistines put themselves in array against Israel: and when they joined battle, Israel was smitten before the Philistines: and they slew of the army in the field about four thousand men. And when the people were come into the camp, the elders of Israel said, Wherefore hath the Lord smitten us today before

141

the Philistines? Let us fetch the ark of the covenant of the Lord out of Shiloh unto us, that, when it cometh among us, it may save us out of the hand of our enemies.

And when the ark of the covenant of the Lord came into the camp, all Israel shouted with a great shout, so that the earth rang again. And when the Philistines heard the noise of the shout, they said, What meaneth the noise of this great shout in the camp of the Hebrews? And they understood that the ark of the Lord was come into the camp. And the Philistines were afraid, for they said, God is come into the camp. And they said, Woe unto us! for there hath not been such a thing heretofore. Woe unto us! who shall deliver us out of the hand of these mighty Gods? these are the Gods that smote the Egyptians with all the plagues in the wilderness. Be strong, and quit yourselves like men, O ye Philistines, that ye be not servants unto the Hebrews, as they have been to you: quit yourselves like men, and fight. And the Philistines fought, and Israel was smitten, and they fled every man into his tent: and there was a very great slaughter; for there fell of Israel thirty thousand footmen. And the ark of God was taken; and the two sons of Eli, Hophni and Phinehas, were slain.

And when Eli heard the noise of the crying, he said, What meaneth the noise of this tumult? And the man came in hastily, and told Eli. And it came to pass, when he made mention of the ark of God, that he fell from off the seat backward by the side of the gate,

and his neck brake, and he died: for he was an old
man, and heavy. And he had judged Israel forty years"
(1 Samuel 4:1-3, 5-11, 14, 18).

1. The Ark of the Covenant

Like the Ark of the Covenant, the African American Church is critical for the survival of the Black community.

a. What role did the Ark of the Covenant have in Israel? (Numbers 10:33-36; Deuteronomy 31:26; Exodus 25:8-9; 1 Samuel 6:1-3, 20–7:2)

b. How did the Ark of the Covenant get returned to Israel? (1 Samuel 13:1-14; 15:25—16:6, 43)

c. Describe the exterior and interior of the Ark of the Covenant. (Exodus 37:1-9; 25:10-22) Describe the table of bread to be offered to God (Exodus 25:23-30; 37:10-16), and the altar. (38:1-7) Describe the interior of the sacred Tent of the Lord's presence. (Exodus 27:20-21; 36:8-38; 38:9-20; Leviticus 24:1-4)

d. How important was the Ark of the Covenant in the lives of the Children of Israel? (Deuteronomy 1:33; Psalm 132:8; Joshua 3:11-17; 4:7, 11, 18; 6:4-12)

e. What role did the house of the Lord play in the training of children? (1 Samuel 1:19-28)

f. SUMMARY QUESTION: Draw as many parallels as you can between the role of the Ark of the Covenant in the lives of the Children of Israel and the African American Church in the history of African Americans.

2. The Temple

In later years, the temple had a similar role as the Ark of the Covenant in the lives of the Children of Israel.

a. What relationship was there between the Ark of the Covenant and the temple? (1 Kings 8:1-13; 2 Chronicles 7:11-22)

143

b. From where did the idea of a temple come? (2 Samuel 7:1-17; 1 Chronicles 28:1-21)

c. Describe the original temple built by Solomon. (2 Chronicles 3:1—4:20)

d. What role did the temple play in the lives of the Children of Israel? (1 Kings 8:22-45; 2 Chronicles 6:12-42)

e. What role did the temple play in the life of Jesus and His earthly family's lives? (Luke 2:22-28, 41-46)

f. SUMMARY QUESTION: Draw as many parallels as you can between the role of the temple in the lives of the Children of Israel and the Black Church in the lives of African Americans today.

3. The New Testament Church

After the death, burial and resurrection of Christ, less emphasis was placed on the physical temple and more on the gathering of believers regardless of the actual physical church.

a. What role did church fellowship have in the lives of 1st century Christians? (Acts 2:1-12, 43-47; 1 Corinthians 1:1-9)

b. What was one purpose of the early church? (Matthew 28:16-20; Acts 2:42-47)

c. What was another purpose of the early church? (1 Corinthians 12:4-12)

d. What was still another purpose of the early church? (1 Corinthians 16:1-4; Romans 15:26-29; 2 Corinthians 8:1-7; Acts 6:1-6)

e. What was yet another purpose of the early church? (2 Timothy 2:15; 3:14-15; Acts 2:42; 13:1; 2 Thessalonians 2:15)

f. SUMMARY QUESTION: Draw as many parallels as possible between the role of church fellowships in the lives of the early Christians and the role of the fellowship of the Black Church in the lives of African Americans today.

4. Biblical Incidents of Church Conflicts

The Bible sheds some light on current conflicts which threaten church unity and survival.

a. How might younger and older people relate to one another in the church? (2 Timothy 1:5; 3:15)

b. What roles have women played in the communities of faith? (2 Kings 2:14-15; Acts 18:1-3, 24-26; 1 Samuel 25:1-42; Judges 4—5)

c. What relationship should exist between the "Haves" and "Haves Nots"? (Acts 2:43-47; 3:1-10; 9:36-42)

d. What types of roles have people with professional training played in the Community of Faith? (Exodus 31:2-11; Ezra 7; Acts 18:24-28)

e. How is it possible for so many different people to achieve unity in the body of Christ? (1 Corinthians 12)

f. SUMMARY QUESTION: In what specific ways do some of the Scriptures in this chapter contradict many traditional attitudes that are prevalent in many Black churches?

5. The Church in the Communities

Historically speaking, the church and the Black church in particular, has always extended itself outside of the walls of the church.

a. Where, in the Bible, does it say for the church to reach outside of its doors? (Matthew 28:18-20)

b. Using Jesus as an example, what is one type of ministry that the church can develop? (Matthew 8:1-3, 5-13, 14, 16-17)

c. Using Jesus as an example, what is another type of ministry that the church can develop? (Mark 6:30-34)

d. Using Jesus as an example, what is still another type of music that a church can develop? (Mark 6:35-44)

e. Using Jesus as an example, what is yet another type of ministry that the church can have? (Luke 8:40-42, 49-56; 7:11-17; John 4:46-54)

f. SUMMARY QUESTION: Draw as many parallels as possible between Jesus' ministry in Galilee and the Black Church's ministry today.

6. CHURCH–BASED MINISTRY

What are the centers of resistance against change in your church? Do they relate to any of the conflicts mentioned in this chapter? Outline a way that your church can resolve these conflicts.

7. PERSONAL APPLICATION

On which side are you? Are you a person who is open to change or one who resists it? If you are a resistor, why do you resist? Is there a valid reason for not changing? This week, take the entire matter to God in prayer.

CHAPTER EIGHT

It was Sunday afternoon. The parking lot across from the church was filled with Bentley Community Church members trying to get ahead of the usual Sunday afternoon traffic jams on Woodward Avenue. Jeffrey and Victor were parked at the church curb, waiting for their parents who were still inside. They were still talking about the pastor's announcement that the city council had voted to allow the university to build a research facility directly across the street from the church.

This would mean that there would be far fewer residences surrounding the church and that many of the elderly African Americans at the church would lose their property to "urban renewal." The pastor announced that the decision had been appealed, and Black community groups would be filing a class action suit. However, he needed people to help him organize a group to attend a hearing about it.

"This action could plunge many of our members into poverty. They can't buy more property at 70 and 80 years of age! I can't understand why the Black community is so apathetic," Jeffrey told Victor. "We couldn't get more than ten people to go down to the first hearing when they voted on the research facility. Some of the very people who would be

losing their property wouldn't even go. How can we get them together to fight this thing?"

"Get together? That'll never happen," Victor said. "Don't you remember what happened last year in the mayoral election? The Black community split right in half, and neither Black candidate won the election."

"But it's not just us, as Black people, and it's not just a local problem. Look at the Supreme Court justices!" Jeffrey continued. "None of them seem to care anything about Black people."

"Yeah. Already, they've been turning over civil rights legislation like pages of a book," Victor added. "By the year 2,000, we may be no better off than we were following Reconstruction at the end of the 19th century."

Just then, Mr. and Mrs. Brown headed toward the car. "Hush," Jeffrey told Victor. "I don't feel like hearing Daddy today, with that stuff about being in the world and not of it." Victor couldn't help being amused at Jeffrey's sudden silence, as his father got into the car and took the driver's seat.

The conflicts expressed in the opening story are not unique. While poverty is a real issue throughout the African American community, the church seems divided in its opinions about the extent to which the Black church should become involved with solving the problem.

Recent data of the U.S. Department of Commerce Bureau of the Census indicate that at least 30.7% (slightly more than 1/3) of African American families live in poverty and this is an in-

crease of 3.2% since 1970. The current rate for white families is 10%, an increase of less than 1%.[1]

While many churches are at the forefront of the political struggle against poverty, a large number are not. The results of a recent Lincoln and Mamiya study tend to support the notion that Black church representatives may be divided in their opinions over the extent to which Christians should become involved.

Out of 2,150 Black church representatives interviewed, 935 (43.5%) had cooperated with civil rights organizations such as the NAACP, while the others had not. Of this same number, only 19.1% had allowed their church buildings to be used as meeting places of such groups.[2] Moreover, political action or awareness groups were not listed among the top nine most common church organizations or auxiliaries.[3] In one of the Lincoln and Mamiya studies, of 1,531 pastors interviewed, only 14% listed civic leadership as being one of their pastoral responsibilities.[4]

However, of 1,894 who responded to the questions, 91% felt that it was all right for clergy to participate in protest marches on civil rights issues, and 91.6% felt that it was all right for them to publicly express their views on such issues.[5] The inability to merge theory with practice (as indicated by some of these statistics) may indicate ambivalence and disunity in opinions over the extent to which Black churches should become involved with achieving economic and political empowerment for the Black community.

In the following sermon, Dr. Hycel Taylor deals with the underlying spiritual issues related to the ambivalence and disunity of the Black church over this issue. He focuses on Jesus' mission on earth, and on the role that forgiveness plays in laying the

149

foundation for the achievement of unity and empowerment among God's people.

FORGIVING, HEALING AND STRATEGIZING

Dr. Hycel Taylor
Luke 4:18-19; 23:34; 1 Peter 1:1-3, 9-10

If one carefully attends to Luke 4, one can locate a movement that is strategically planned and that is to be consummated in a calculated period of three years.

In this passage, Jesus stands in a synagogue and outlines His plan as follows:

  a. Preach the narrative of God's liberation to the poor.
  b. Heal the brokenhearted.
  c. Deliver the captives.
  d. Recover sight to the blind.
  e. Set at liberty those who are bruised.
  f. Announce that the time has come when the Lord will save His people.

Then, in Luke the 23rd chapter, in one of the last phrases that Jesus would utter before His death, Jesus presents the summation of the movement. First Peter the second chapter is a post-Easter rehearsal of the movement which had taken place over a span of three years.

Let's begin our exploration of this movement with a study of the statement, "Father, forgive them; for they know not what they do." On one level, this passionate and poignant cry of Jesus could be interpreted as a prophetic, self-centered plea regarding the personal injury He is experiencing at the hands of ungrateful people who are inflicting undeserved punishment upon Him.

150

This is a popular interpretation because most people know how it feels to be renounced, rejected, criticized and ostracized. Many have been abused, battered and beaten by people to whom they have given their total selves. This type of treatment is particularly painful when a person has given all that the person has. Black people who are victims of the ravages of racism might hear it in this way because Black people know that mistreatment is a demeaning and a demoralizing experience. It is an experience that terrorizes egos and tramples one's pride into the dust. Black people know what that is like.

Abuse Makes a Mockery of One's Principleness. It robs one of all that constitutes the African American race as a beautiful race with extraordinary possibilities. Abuse belittles and degrades people, and it robs African Americans of the integrity of the African heritage. Worst of all it profanes the African American spirit, the spirit which Black ancestors held sacred, the spirit that has empowered Black people to look into the future and articulate goals for liberation.

Therefore, most Black people cannot blame Jesus for expressing His personal disappointment and disillusionment, as He cried, "Father, forgive them; for they know not what they do." However, after a closer examination of the passage and of the life of Christ, one must ask whether Jesus is stating disappointment, or whether His response is one of a selfless martyr who is utterly detached from His own persecution, oblivious to His own pain, but who is surveying the sickness and sadism, madness and masochism, divisiveness and destructiveness of a people. It is His own people, locked into the pathology of self-punishment and self-oppression. Is it not His vision of the condition of His people which pricks His spirit and causes Him to appeal to God?

Visualize the Scene. Jesus, placed high on a cruel crucifix, frowns at the press of Calvary, and views the awesome Roman citadel surrounded with centurions. The centurions have the primary purpose of protecting Roman property while prodding the oppressed Jewish masses to promote their own persecution.

151

Yet Jesus could not bear to see the innocent and the ignorant of His pitiful people engaged in sickness and self-genocide. Visualize Him saying, "Father, let's get on with this. Let's finish this task for which I have come. Let me die quickly because they are a tragic, disgusting, and pathetic sight. I can't bear it."

Another way of viewing this scene on Calvary would be to take the sentimentality out of it. An alternative would be to see it as the first phase of the last stage of the movement that Jesus set forth in Luke the fourth chapter.

The Cross is meaningless unless it is viewed in light of the goals and aims that were essential for the overall strategy of Jesus. Jesus' Seven Last Words are merely a living moment summing up the meaning of His movement, with "Forgive" being the first phase of it. This chapter does not deal with the remaining six words. However, a reading of them would reveal the coherent structure of Jesus' strategy. This chapter focuses on forgiveness.

Forgiveness. First of all it is necessary to demystify the meaning of forgiveness by understanding it in light of Jesus' goals and objectives. In this light, forgiveness has meaning only in relation to a situation in which there is no separation between God and humankind. It is a relationship to the divine in which there is no separation.

The first commandment speaks of it more clearly than anything: "Thou shalt love the Lord thy God with all of thy heart, and with all thy soul, and with all thy mind…love thy neighbor as thyself" (Matthew 22:37, 39). This would mean that humankind as a whole is in unity. There is no brokenness. Wherever there is love, there is also a state of unity. There is no brokenness in it.

People who are in love are easy to recognize because they are so close to one another. They don't want any separation between themselves. They are in a state that is similar to the original state of divine and human oneness—the relationship between God and humankind before the Fall.

152

However, the need for forgiveness presumes that the original state of divine and human oneness was disrupted. It was torn apart. That destruction was caused by sin, because sin actually means separation. It means alienation. It means brokenness.

Sin is more than the issue of where, when, how and with whom one sleeps, for example. Sexual immorality is merely a manifestation of sin. Sin itself is whatever separates a person from God. Forgiveness has to do with the action of atonement to restore unity with God and with one another. Forgiveness is the action of love that removes the barriers that disrupt the original unity between humans and God.

Forgiveness and the Movement. What does all of this have to do with the Jesus movement? Initiating the action of forgiveness is the first phase of the last stage of Jesus' movement for the liberation of oppressed people. The oppressed have no power to effect their liberation. The oppressed, wherever they are, cannot effect their liberation unless they can protect themselves against aggression from within and from outside. At all costs, they must avoid internal disintegration.

A Visual Image of Disunity. Let's use a visual image to explain what this means. If one could examine one of the finest apples that one could get, one would discover that the apple has unity. It has integrity. It is centered in itself. It has power. It can stand against any other fruit in the fruit world, without apology, because an apple is an apple. One can visualize this perfect apple.

However, if a person took the same apple, laid it on a desk and, with a butcher knife, sliced the apple in two, immediately one would see that the apple loses some of its dignity and power. If it is sliced a third time, it would fall into four pieces. If one were to remove the seeds from this same apple and scatter them, the apple would again lose much of its power. Suppose the sliced apple segments were placed among oranges and then one said to the apple, "Look at yourself. Look how bad you look. Look how you're all divided up."

What if a person then took the same apple, and with syringes, shot drugs into the apple? What if the person injected the drugs into one piece at a time. Then, after pumping drugs into it, the person injected a disease like AIDS, to tear the apple apart. Then the same person might move part of the apple to the west side of the table and another part to the south side of the table. Then the person might tell the west side part of the apple that it is better than the south side part of the apple. Then, after moving the parts around, the person might take knives and give them to the apple parts and say, "Finish yourself off! Kill yourself! Destroy yourself! Get rid of yourself! Do it! You do it!"

Can't you hear Jesus crying, "Father, forgive them; for they know not what they do. Father, look at them, look at them out there, all divided. They are all over the place!" In this context, forgiveness would mean bringing back together that which has been torn apart.

Another Visual Image. Let's examine another visual image for even more clarity. Once my family and I were traveling through Sandusky, Ohio. Sandusky has an outdoor zoo. A person can drive through that zoo and view the animals without leaving the car. The animals come to the car and a person can feed them out of the window of the car. It's a joyful experience! However, something very ugly caught my eye when I was there.

It was a cage in that zoo, a cone–shaped cage. Inside the cage was a family of wolves. They all looked alive. There was a mama wolf, a papa wolf and little baby wolves. There was even a cousin wolf. In fact there were plenty of cousin wolves. The wolves all shared a common heritage. They obviously shared a common color. They all seemed to look alike. There were many variations but, in the main, they were wolves of the same family.

We were there all day, but the zoo keeper did not come and feed them breakfast. No, he didn't do that. I noticed that at lunchtime he still didn't come. Then late in the evening, when they were all very hungry, from a mile away one could see the zoo keeper coming. Obviously the wolves knew his pattern, because as they saw him coming, they became very happy and began to jump up and down. If they could have talked they might have said, "Here comes the zoo keeper! Here comes the zoo keeper!"

When the zoo keeper finally got there, I thought to myself, "I know this zoo keeper is going to be a kind zoo keeper. I know what he is going to do."

I believed this because he had a bucket of horse meat, and I expected this "kind" zoo keeper to open the cage and throw the horse meat out and say, "Come wolves and eat!"

But he didn't do that. I watched carefully and I noticed that the zoo keeper waited until the wolves were happy to see him. Then the zoo keeper went up to the cage and, rather than open it up, he made a small door at the bottom of the cage. Into that little door he threw the meat, but not the whole bucket of horse meat! He didn't do that. He threw in one piece of meat and then watched the wolves fight over it, killing one another. He stood there with his arms folded and watched them run over little baby wolves, over the mama wolf, and over the papa wolf. It was wolf on wolf crime!

After a while, a bad big black wolf finally overcame all of the other wolves and got that one piece of meat. Then this wolf rushed off to the side, fended off all of the other wolves, and ate the meat. The zoo keeper stood there with his arms folded and, as soon as the wolves were all terrorized by this one big wolf and were hungrily waiting, he pulled the cage door open again and threw in one more piece. I watched as the pack of wolves shifted and ran to the other side with all of them tearing one another apart. Even the big bad black wolf, who had already had a piece of meat, participated. He didn't know whether to leave what he had or run over there. He was confused and in-between.

Finally I said to myself, these wolves are behaving just like us. Why are they fighting over this one little piece of meat? Why are they trying to kill one another over this? Why can't they sit down and formulate a strategy? If the wolves knew what Jesus meant by forgiveness, if they knew what it meant to remove bar-

155

riers and pull things back together, if they knew what it meant to learn how to love one another in the midst of struggle, they would sit down together and formulate a strategy. They would suffer a little of the torture of hunger, but on the next day, they would have their act together.

Visualize them now, calling a summit meeting. They would call this group over here and that group over there. They would call the family together. Can't you see them getting up the next morning and implementing a strategy that would overcome their problem once and for all?

Visualize them saying, "When the zoo keeper comes, jump up and down. Make him feel like he is somebody. Carry on like the crazy fools you have been acting like all year.

"However, when he gets here and comes to the cage to pull open the door, don't go for the meat! Go for the zoo keeper! Take the keys and eat the zoo keeper! Tear him apart. Then open the door to the cage, walk out of here and stay out!"

As I mentioned in the beginning of this story, the wolves remind me of us. The wolves in that cage remind me of the state of affairs among Chicagoans, a few years ago, following the death of Mayor Harold Washington. There was one piece of meat called "mayor." I watched us kill one another over that one piece of meat.

However, Jesus is correct. People must learn how to forgive one another. People must be able to set aside pain. People must learn to love one another. African Americans must learn how to love one another. African Americans must learn how to walk together. Black people must not allow themselves to be separated into pieces and pushed to different sides of the table. We must not kill one another over one piece of meat.

Forgiving, Unifying, and Strategizing. We the people have met our enemy! We must realize that the enemy wants to conquer us! We must understand that the reason why the enemy spends so much time conquering us is that the enemy fears us.

Christians are a chosen race. We are royal people. We are a holy nation. We must rise up and walk like one! We must talk like one! We must think like one! We must walk together! We must overcome it together! If we forgive one another and unify, with the power of God, we can select a good candidate and put him or her into office. We can overcome the enemy, but we can't do it in a state of divisiveness! Can't you hear Jesus crying, "Father, forgive them, Father, forgive them. Father, forgive them! They are ignorant! They don't know what they're doing!"

BIBLE STUDY APPLICATION

Instructions: The following exercises provide the opportunity to study some of the truths presented by Dr. Taylor more closely. The exercises draw parallels between conditions in the Jewish community during Jesus' ministry and conditions in the African American community today. They illustrate the applications of forgiveness and the importance of strategizing.

"The spirit of the Lord is upon me, because he hath anointed me to preach to gospel to the poor; he hath sent me to heal the brokenhearted, to preach deliverance to the captives, and recovering of sight to the blind, to set at liberty them that are bruised, To preach the acceptable year of the Lord.

Then said Jesus, Father, forgive them; for they know not what they do. And they parted his raiment, and cast lots" (Luke 4:18-19; 23:34).

"Peter, an apostle of Jesus Christ, to the strangers scattered throughout Pontus, Galatia, Cappadocia, Asia, and Bithynia, Elect according to the foreknowledge of God the Father, through sanctification of the Spirit,

unto obedience and sprinkling of the blood of Jesus Christ: Grace unto you, and peace, be multiplied. Blessed be the God and Father of our Lord Jesus Christ, which according to his abundant mercy hath begotten us again unto a lively hope by the resurrection of Jesus Christ from the dead,

Receiving the end of your faith, even the salvation of your souls. Of which salvation the prophets have inquired and searched diligently, who prophesied of the grace that should come unto you" (1 Peter 1:1-3, 9-10).

1. The Roman Empire

Just as the zoo keeper's actions (in Dr. Taylor's illustration) brought about fighting among the wolves, so the actions of the Roman Empire resulted in fighting among the Jews.

a. What was one way in which most Jews experienced the presence of the Roman Empire in their lives? (Luke 2:1-7)

b. What was another way in which Jews experienced the presence of the Roman Empire in their lives? (Matthew 22:15-22; Mark 12:13-17; Luke 20:19-26; 23:5)

c. What was yet another way in which Jews felt the presence of the Roman Empire in their lives? (Matthew 27:1-2, 15, 26-31, 57-58; 28:11-19)

d. What is another, somewhat more subtle way in which Jews experienced and responded to the controlling presence of the Roman Empire in their lives? (John 19:12-6; Luke 23:1-3)

e. A number of Jews became "publicans," or tax collectors for the Roman Empire. How did this lead to conflicts between them and the general masses of Jews? (Luke 3:3-14; 19:1-8; 5:27-32; Matthew 5:46-48; 9:10-11; 11:19)

f. SUMMARY QUESTION: Are there any parallels between the role that the Romans played in the Jewish community and the role that the larger American society plays in the lives of African Americans today? Explain.

2. A Community Divided

The Jews at the time of Christ were divided into pieces just as the apple described by Dr. Taylor was severed into pieces.

a. In what ways were Jews exploiting other Jews financially? Why might they have felt the need to do this? (Luke 3:3-14; 19:1-8; Matthew 5:47-48)

b. In what ways did Jews use religion to establish social classes among themselves? Why might they have felt a psychological need for these hierarchies? (Matthew 15:1-9; 23:1-28; Luke 7:36-39; 18:10-14)

c. In what ways did the Jewish religious Sanhedrin Council allow itself to become a "police force" for the Roman Empire? Why might they have felt the necessity to play this role? (John 18:12-14; Matthew 26:47-48, 57, 59-64; 27:1-2)

d. What was a central issue that pitted one Jew against another? (Matthew 12:23-27) Why might this issue have become so important?

e. What evidence is there that some Jews were not above joining with Romans in carrying out various forms of corruption? Why might they have felt the need to do this? (Matthew 27:27-44; 28:11-15)

f. SUMMARY QUESTION: Compare and contrast the economic, political, social and religious divisions among the Jews at the time of Christ, with similar divisions among African Americans today. Are there any similarities in the role that oppressors have played in perpetuating these divisions?

3. The Herods

In some ways, the Herod family, which descended from the Jewish Idumaens, behaved as a "big bad wolf" among the Jews.

a. Herod was not a personal, but a family name. What

evidence is there of this in Scripture? (Matthew 2:1-4, 19-23; 14:1-4; Luke 23:5-12)

b. Over what territories did the various Herods rule? (Luke 3:1-2; Matthew 2:22)

c. What was a primary objective of one of the first Herods? (Matthew 2:1-4, 19-23) Why might the achievement of this objective seemed so important to Herod?

d. What was the primary objective of Herod Antipas? (Luke 13:31-32) Why might he have chosen to "pass the buck" rather than act on his feelings? (Luke 23:6-15)

e. What was Herod Antipas' general lifestyle and management style? (Matthew 14:1-12)

f. SUMMARY QUESTION: Are there any similarities at all between Herod and "big bad wolves" among African Americans today? Explain.

4. Forgiveness

Dr. Taylor states that forgiveness of God and forgiveness of one another can bring about healing and unity.

a. In what ways can partaking in the Lord's Supper promote both forgiveness and unity? (1 Corinthians 11:23-33)

b. Summarize what the following Scriptures say about the forgiveness of God. (Romans 8; Colossians 2:13; John 3:18; 5:24)

c. How has the Lord provided for sins in the daily lives of believers to be forgiven? (1 Corinthians 11:31, 32; 1 John 1:9)

d. What is the relationship between forgiveness among God and human beings and the forgiveness among human beings? (Matthew 6:14-5; 18:21-35; Mark 11:25-26)

e. How does forgiveness promote unity among people? (2 Corinthians 2:5-11; Ephesians 4:31—5:20; Colossians 3:13-17)

f. SUMMARY QUESTION: Is it possible for forgiveness to begin within churches and extend into communities, resulting in unity throughout the Black community? If so, can such a unifying process have political ramifications? Explain.

5. Unifying and Strategizing

Dr. Taylor states that once unity is achieved, people are in a position to plan and deal with oppressors more effectively.

a. What is one example of how unity helped a group to fight a battle together? (Joshua 6)

b. What is another example of how unity helped a group to deal with an oppressor? (Judges 4)

c. What is an example of how unity helped a group to deal with a crisis? (Ruth 1—4)

e. What is another example of how unity helped a group to deal with oppression? (Acts 12:1-17)

d. What is another example of how unity helped a group to creatively deal with the effects of oppression? (Acts 2:43-47; 4:32-37)

f. SUMMARY QUESTION: Are there any lessons that African Americans can learn from these stories? Are there any special implications for the Black church? Are there any implications for unity among people of African descent throughout the world?

6. CHURCH–BASED MINISTRY

Should the local church become involved in voter registration? Should it become involved with local school boards? What about local and national elections? What would forgiveness and unity have to do with it?

7. PERSONAL APPLICATION

Are you struggling with an unforgiving spirit within yourself? If so, review the Scriptures cited in this chapter, and go to the Lord in prayer. Ask Him to help you in your weakness (2 Corinthians 12:9).

161

CHAPTER NINE

It was an awesome sight, wrote Cindy on her note pad. The cheerleaders, dressed in their uniforms, and the two basketball teams, dressed in their uniforms, were all kneeling at the center of the basketball court and praying, while gang members and other people from the community stood in the bleachers, watching. The gym was filled to capacity.

Cindy a reporter, was writing a story on the opening of the playoffs for the Christian Basketball League. Earlier, she had interviewed Coach Vance, founder of the league, and the coach of the True Vine Community Church team. She watched Mr. Vance as he skirted around the rim of the court, occasionally calling out to the players.

Before the game he had told her how long it took him to convince the city's recreation department to allow this league to use the gym free of charge, and how he had solicited help from local businesses to purchase the uniforms. At first the city was afraid to allow too many community people into the gym at one time, for fear that this would lead to gang violence.

"No one would believe that at least ten people on our team are former gang members. They accepted Christ this year and now they are studying their

> *Bibles at local churches throughout city," Coach Vance told Cindy, beaming.*
>
> *Cindy didn't believe it until she saw it with her own eyes. By now, the Christian Basketball League had spread to churches throughout the city. "I've got to get a shot of this audience," she whispered to her photographer, as the prayer was ending. Her eyes perused the crowd, falling on gang members, here and there, dressed in their gang attire and waiting for the game to begin.*

This case study presents an example of a very innovative program which takes the church into the community in order to creatively win people for Christ. Eric Lincoln and Lawrence Mamiya, in "The Black Church in the African American Experience," presented the results of surveys of over 2,000 Black churches throughout the United States, in which, among other topics, they asked about the nature and extent of outreach programs in local churches.[1] Unfortunately, the results of their research do not reflect widespread use of innovative programs to reach the unsaved. There seems to be relatively little interaction between the church and the community surrounding it. One way that churches might interact with the community might be by cooperating with other agencies to improve the quality of life for African Americans.

While about 50% of 619 churches contacted reported cooperating with civil rights organizations, 32.5% reported no cooperation at all, and less than 1% interacted with any type of social agency other than those involving senior citizens.[2]

Another means of interacting with people from the community would be to participate in government–funded programs which prohibit discrimination based on religious preference (in the program itself, not in the church). These programs could be used to make initial contacts which might lead to opportunities to share the Gospel. However, only 6.4% of 2,150 churches contacted participated in any government-funded programs. Another means of reaching out to the community would be through community service-oriented programs or recreational ones such as Coach Vance's basketball league. However, only 3.5% of the 2,150 churches contacted had such programs.[3]

In the following sermon, Tom Skinner presents ideas that local churches can use to reach communities surrounding churches. He presents a variety of nontraditional strategies for winning people to Christ.

THE CHURCH IN THE COMMUNITY

Tom Skinner
Matthew 28:16-20

One of the things that keeps the church from being a voice in the community is that the Church doesn't do the things of God in locations where the world will be able to see it. Most Christians reserve all of their teaching and preaching and testifying for one another.

The problem is that Christians tend to shy away from people of the world because they fear they might lose their testimonies.

There are many creative ways for the people of God to make an impact on communities. All they need to do is pull off restrictive shackles. The Word of God says not to be of the world, but to be in it.

165

Jesus said Christians should be lights. The function of a light is to scatter darkness. However, what God's people have been doing is taking out a flashlight at noon and singing, "This little light of mine, I'm gonna let it shine." Light is not needed in the sun. Light is needed where it is dark. That's where God's people have to be a voice. That's where we have to exert influence. We must go to the darkest places and turn the light on.

Bar Ministries. In New York I train people to do bar ministries. People don't go to bars to drink. They go there to socialize. Bars are the great communication places of the world. Drinking at home is less expensive than drinking in a bar. People go to bars because they are lonely. If people go to bars to talk, why can't Christians supply the conversation? We can educate people to do that in Christian education.

In New York, about five or six brothers locate places where ladies of the evening take breaks between their customers. These brothers go to these coffee shops and restaurants and talk to them. When one of the ladies says she'd like to stay but doesn't have time, the brother says, how much for your time? She asks, what do you mean? He repeats, how much for your time? Then she tells him. Then he goes into his pocket and takes out that amount of money and gives it to her. Then they continue to talk. She wants to go, but he tells her that he has paid for the time so she has to talk. Then he explains who Christ is to her.

Community Gatherings. Next we must consider some things that make up a community. That is, when people gather in communities, we find churches, banks, schools, ball games, supermarkets, hospitals, beauty shops, barber shops, laundromats, and basketball courts. These are all places where people of God need to appear. For example, some need to join the Democratic club in the neighborhood. Some need to join the Republican club. Christians don't necessarily join them because they are Democrats or Republicans, but because they are God's people and God's people need to be there.

God's People in Office. God's people need to run for office. They need to be on the city council, representing the kingdom of God. They need to be in the state legislature, representing the kingdom of God. When issues arise, God's people need to stand up and present God's point of view. However, Christians tend to run from all of those things, as though politics is dirty. But God has called them to go where it is dirty. These are all ways that God's people can have an impact on the community.

The Parish Community. There was a time when churches referred to themselves as parishes. They even named their churches after their parishes. For example, there was a St. Andrew's Parish and a St. Andrew's church. There was St. Phillip's Parish and a St. Phillip's church. The church saw their parish community as their territory for ministry. Their community was the place where God called them to be a light in darkness, and sheep among wolves. Today Christians need to return to the idea of doing sabotage in a neighborhood in the name of Jesus!

There has probably been a meeting some place where the devil and his angels have remarked that they noticed that wherever they are, the people of God don't come. They probably concluded that the best way to take over the neighborhood is to tell the people of God that Satan and his demons are everywhere. They knew that if they convinced Christians that they were everywhere the Christians might leave a whole neighborhood alone!

Then Satan got to work. He started putting up "no trespassing" signs. Maybe that is how Christians lost their territories! We have not influencing the world for Christ, because we have been running from it.

The Schools. Take the schools, for instance. What's the favorite expression of the people of God about schools? "They took prayer out of the schools. Godless schools."

However, what the law really says is that the state cannot prescribe a prayer for students. Nothing in the law forbids praying. If the children we educate through the church's Christian

Education programs are being taught how to represent Christ in school, prayer will not leave school. Why hasn't it dawned on us that the answer to getting in the schools is through the children? If we educate our children, they will take Christ to school.

The enemy has taken our children. He has taken our young people and is killing them. However, we keep saying that we can't go out and get them. We're unwilling to go out into the community and do battle for the lives of our young people! We keep saying we can't go out in the world!

In high schools all over the country, principals are looking for anyone who can help them with the children. At one time, they warned Christians to be careful about what was said. However, now they don't care what a person says, if it helps. Children are burning the schools down. People are so confused, particularly those who run the schools.

A school board in Maryland voted to distribute condoms and contraceptives in the schools, without parental consent. However, the same school board supports the rule that if a child has a headache and needs an aspirin, the child must secure written permission from parents in order to get the aspirin. But they don't ask for permission to give the child a contraceptive.

When I asked the chairman of the school board about it, and whether any Christians had expressed a view on it, he said not one Christian came down there and presented his/her viewpoint. Christians cannot have influence if they are not represented at the school board. That's where the people of God must be. There is no place that excludes the people of God from exerting influence. All we need is a strategy for making an impact.

Full-Time Christian Work. It is an error to separate everything into worldly and spiritual and always to want to be where it's spiritual. Along this same vein, we have created what we call full-time Christian work. What is full-time Christian work? If a person is not in "full–time" Christian work, does it mean his or her work as a Christian is only part–time? Is he/she only serving the Lord part of the time? Most Christians view their jobs as a

168

way to pay their bills. They hope there is enough time left from their jobs to do something for Jesus. They don't consider their job as a mission field. They don't consider their job as a place of ministry. When most people talk about full-time Christian work, they think of leaving their jobs and hoping other Christians will raise money to support them. However, the company you work for is already paying you to be a witness on your jobs. They even provide pensions and health care plans.

Confining one's work to the church represents a mentality that we must change. Thinking that way is a habit—a bad habit. In order to change a bad habit, a person has to cultivate a good habit to replace the bad habit.

Boldness. When Jesus said to go into all the world and preach the Gospel, He meant to go into all the world and preach the Gospel! This means abandoning the notion that some things are secular and others are spiritual. There is only one world. There is not a secular world and a spiritual world. There is one world and God is at work in it.

In the New Testament, whenever a phrase appears about the fullness of the Holy Spirit, it is always followed by a word about boldness. One of the characteristics of being filled with the Spirit is boldness. When we are filled with the Spirit, we don't need to apologize to the world.

One of the great problems Christians face is that we confine the word "ministry" to the preacher. We see ministers as people who wear clerical collars and have "reverend" in front of their names. However, the Bible says that God has called all of us to do the work of the ministry. In fact, according to the Scripture the function of the pastor is to equip the saints for the work of the ministry. This means that the saints do the ministry. The function of the pastor is to equip them. The saints are in the community. If they are equipped, they can do ministry wherever they are.

Reaching the World Through Children. Children provide another example of the way the Church can influence the world.

169

For example, why not invite the parents of your children to your home? Even invite individual gang members to your home. Some people shy away from that. However, people don't understand that only one side of a child is in a gang. On the other side they are still children. On this other side, they are no different from your children or anyone else's children.

They have the same problems and emotions. They are frightened teenagers whom no one has bothered to love. The reason they congregate in gangs is that they believe that gang members need one another. They believe no one else cares about them. That is how they got into the gang in the first place.

Loving People. The real secret of ministry is loving people. A person doesn't necessarily have to tell another person anything. All s/he needs to do is love them. Christians tend to think that witnessing is always telling someone something. However, sometimes it is just caring about people. Caring opens doors for witnessing. In order to share Christ with someone, a Christian must first build trust. Christians can turn their homes into places of ministry. Christian homes can be places of refuge where people can come and feel comfortable.

An example of this is a friend of mine in Philadelphia. He has five sons. Every Saturday he has open house where his sons bring their friends to the house. They have barbecues. He and his wife cook. At one of these barbecues, one of his sons' friends was noticing that he and his wife were in the kitchen while they were cooking, cuddling and playing with one another.

One of the boys asked his son if the lady in the kitchen was really his father's wife or his "old lady." The child was confused. First of all, he didn't know anyone who was married. Most people in his neighborhood just "shacked up." Secondly he rarely, if ever, saw married people being affectionate. Most married people he knew never looked like they liked one another. That is why he was confused about what was happening that day. Unless a person has a model, a scene like that is confusing.

Occupying Until Jesus Comes. Jesus said to "occupy until I come." There are some Black Muslims who can do this better than Christians. In Washington, D.C. the Muslim brothers chose a block that had the worst drug traffic in the neighborhood. Four Muslims stood on one corner, four stood on another, and twelve stood on another. They just stood and talked to one another. Then a drug pusher and a person who was going to purchase the drugs would come along. The Muslim brothers would then walk over to where they stood and stand there. They didn't say anything to them, they just stood there. The drug pushers would see them and move away.

However, the Muslim brothers would go on over to where they moved. Finally the drug pusher would ask the Muslims what they were trying to do. The Muslims told them they just wanted to be near them. The point is, Jesus said, "Occupy until I come!"

After only 35 days, no more drugs were sold on that street. That is what Jesus meant. The Church must be in the neighborhood! It must occupy until He comes.

One of the things the Church needs to do is stop considering evangelism as a program. Evangelism is a relationship. Establish relationships with others. That's really all evangelism is. It's talking about Jesus. It's not a program.

Being Comfortable with Blackness. African Americans are the only people who try to deny their cultural heritage of Blackness in the name of Jesus. Many African Americans believe that when they become Christians, they suddenly become faceless and colorless. In other words, Black Christians become like Europeans. Many feel it is only appropriate to deny one's Blackness. However, Black people need to understand that there is a reason why God created people the way they are. It makes no sense to deny that. A rose does not deny being a rose in the presence of lilies! Lilies don't deny being lilies in the presence of roses! In other words, a person is who God made the person to be! Christians must get away from denying their Blackness in the name of Jesus. Blackness is a means that God can use to

171

reach Black people.

Black Christians must start finding themselves as Black people, in the Scriptures. Then they must show other Black people that they are there in Scripture. There are some excellent books written about the presence of Black people in the Bible. Reverend Walter McCray's book, *The Black Presence in the Bible* even gives you the history of Black tribes in the Bible. Such books are written by born-again believers. In reaching Black people for Christ, we need to get some understanding of that.

It is also essential to understand that we are worse off now than we were in the days of dejure segregation. Genocidal homicide is greater now than it ever was during the period of lynchings. Black people are in trouble. God's Black people cannot afford to disconnect themselves from their Blackness, if they are going to win people to Christ. The trouble is, too many of us believe that God has saved us from the very folk we are called to win!

Summary. This chapter has dealt with the challenge of taking the Black church into the community. It has presented several innovative strategies for witnessing for Christ in nontraditional settings. It is hoped that, as a result of this chapter, Black churches everywhere will be better equipped to carry out the divine commission (Matthew 28:16-20).

BIBLE STUDY APPLICATION

Instructions: The following exercises provide the opportunity to study how the apostles followed Jesus' instructions in Matthew 28:16-20. The first five exercises consist of short answer "discovery" questions and a summary question. The sixth exercise is an opportunity to apply principles learned from this chapter to a church-based ministry. The seventh exercise is for personal application.

"Then the eleven disciples went away into Galilee, into a mountain where Jesus had appointed them. And when they saw him, they worshipped him: but some doubted. And Jesus came and spake unto them, saying, All power is given unto me in heaven and in earth. Go ye therefore, and teach all nations, baptizing them in the name of the Father, and of the Son, and of the Holy Ghost: Teaching them to observe all things whatsoever I have commanded you: and, lo, I am with you always, even unto the end of the world. Amen" (Matthew 28:16-20).

1. Peter

Peter spread the Gospel in nontraditional places (outside the temple walls).

a. What was one environment in which Peter spread the Gospel? (Acts 2)

b. What was another environment where Peter spread the Gospel? How did he do it? (Acts 9:32–43)

c. What was another environment where Peter spread the Gospel? How did he do it? (Acts 10:1-48)

d. What was another environment where Peter spread the Gospel? (Acts 12:1-11)

e. What is yet anther environment where Peter spread the Gospel? How did he do it? (Acts 8:4-25)

f. SUMMARY: Draw some parallels between environments in which Peter found himself spreading the Gospel and environments in which Christians find themselves today. Can Christians learn anything from Peter's experiences?

2. Philip

Philip spread the Gospel outside of the walls of the temple.

a. What is one environment where Philip spread the Gospel? (Acts 8:4-13)

b. What is another environment where Philip spread the Gospel? How did he do it? (Acts 8:26-40)

c. Azotus is the Greek word for Ashdod. Based on the following Scriptures what type reputation did Ashdod have? What are some of the prophecies that had been made against it? What did Philip do there? (Acts 8:40; Joshua 11:21-22; 1 Samuel 5:1-8; Nehemiah 4:7-9; Zechariah 9:1-8; Zephaniah 2:1-4)

d. What is yet another environment in which Philip spread the Gospel? (Acts 8:40; 10:24-28)

e. What is one unusual situation where Philip helped the other disciples in their spreading of the Gospel? (Acts 6)

f. SUMMARY: Draw some parallels between environments in which Philip found himself spreading the Gospel and environments in which Christians must spread the Gospel today. Can Christians learn anything from Philip's experiences?

3. John

John spread the Gospel outside the temple walls.

a. What is one environment where John spread the Gospel? (Acts 4)

b. What is another environment where John spread the Gospel? (Acts 8)

c. What is one way in which John continues to spread the Gospel throughout the world today? (Revelation 1:1-4, 9-11)

d. What was one way in which John suffered as a result of his participation in spreading the Good News? (Acts 12)

e. What was another way in which John suffered as a result of his involvement in spreading the Good News? (Revelation 1:9)

f. SUMMARY: Draw some parallels between circumstances surrounding John as he spread the Good News and circumstances surrounding African Americans as they spread the Good News today. Are there any guidelines that can be gleaned from these situations?

4. Paul

Paul was not one of the original apostles. However, he carried the Gospel outside of the walls of the temple.

a. What is one of the first places where Paul spread the Good News? (Acts 9:26-31) What type of reception did he get?

b. What is another "nontraditional" place where Paul spread the Good News? (Acts 13:4-12)

c. In what other "nontraditional" place did Paul spread the Gospel? (Acts 14:1-6)

d. In what other "nontraditional" place did Paul spread the Good News? (Acts 14:8-20)

e. In what other "nontraditional" place did Paul spread the Good News? (Acts 16:16-40)

f. SUMMARY: Draw parallels between the environments in which Paul spread the Good News and environments where Christians must spread the Gospel today. Are there any guidelines that can be gleaned from these examples?

5. Jesus

Jesus Himself carried the news of the kingdom of God outside the temple walls.

a. What is one "nontraditional" place where Jesus spread the news of the kingdom of God? (Matthew 5:1-11)

b. In what other "nontraditional" setting did Jesus spread the Good News? (Matthew 7:5-13) How did He do it?

c. In what other "nontraditional" setting did Jesus spread the Good News? How did He do it? (Matthew 7:14-22)

d. In what other "nontraditional" setting did Jesus spread the Good News? (Matthew 8:28-34)

e. In what other "nontraditional" setting did Jesus spread the Good News? (Matthew 12:1-8)

f. SUMMARY: Draw parallels between the environments where Jesus spread the Good News and environments where Christians must spread the Good News today.

6. CHURCH–BASED MINISTRY

Consider the community in which your church is located. Make a list of nontraditional places where Christians can and must spread the Good News. Then list some strategies that can be developed for implementing this goal. Consult Tom Skinner's article for specific ideas.

7. PERSONAL APPLICATION

During the course of the week, in what places do you spend time (other than the local church)? In what sense might these places be "nontraditional" settings for spreading the Gospel? How can you spread the Good News in these places? Consult Tom Skinner's article for specific ideas.

CHAPTER TEN

Cookie kicked a beer can out of her way as she slowly walked toward the grocery store. As usual, her mother had gone to work and had left her a couple of dollars to purchase her dinner. She had just gotten home from school and found the money on the table with a note. She felt so lonely.

As she made her way toward the grocery store, a feeling of terror suddenly struck her heart as a man ran down the steps of one of the tenement houses and cut in front of her. Immediately her mind flashed back to the night she was raped. It had been just before dark, on a night like this. Her mother was at work, as usual, and she was going to the store to buy something for dinner.

As she walked down the street today, she looked around her and hated every man she saw. In her pocket, she carried a butcher knife and some mace. "I'll kill the first one that comes near me," she thought. Suddenly her thoughts were interrupted by what sounded like angels singing in the yard behind the house she was passing. From behind her, she heard a familiar voice calling her name. She looked around just in time to see Janet, her friend. "Cookie!" Janet called. "Come with me. I'm going to Mrs. Stephen's after-school Bible study. I've been wanting to invite you."

At first Cookie thought this was silly and childish, but she went along. Something within her seemed to be attracting her to the angelic voices she heard. When she got to the backyard Bible study, she listened closely as Mrs. Stephens talked about the death, burial and resurrection of Jesus Christ. Mrs. Stephens explained how Jesus had been abused and mistreated, but He died so that others might live. As Cookie listened, she began to be drawn to Jesus. For the first time in her life, she believed that she had a personal Friend she could trust to love and protect her.

When she left the Bible study and headed for the grocery store, Cookie felt like she was a new person, ready to face life again.

This case study is an example of an innovative method that one Christian woman used to reach neighborhood children and teenagers to Christ. Programs such as this are so important. For some people, a backyard Bible class represents their first contact with the Gospel of Jesus Christ.

It is not uncommon today to meet African American families in which there are no church members. This is particularly common among single-parent families where often the head of the household is under 18 years of age. Therefore, there is a particular need to reach young people.

A study by Eric Lincoln and Lawrence Mamiya provides statistical data reflecting this need. The results of their survey of 2,150 churches reflected an average total membership of 390 per church. In urban settings, however, the number was much higher, at 479 members per church. However, of this total, youth constituted only 26% of the congregation. For urban churches, the figure was slightly less (25%), and for rural churches, it was much higher (32%).[1]

The results of the Lincoln/Mamiya study also reflect a need to reach Black men. Out of the total average membership of 390 per church, Black males comprised only 18% of the membership. In urban churches, the percentage was slightly higher, at 19%, and in rural churches, it was 18%. This indicates a general need for evangelism in all churches, but there is a particular need to reach young people and Black men for the Lord.

In the following article, Crawford Loritts presents the need for evangelism, and the urgency for Christians to be able to go into all of the world with the Gospel.

WINNING PEOPLE

Crawford W. Loritts, Jr.
Mark 16:14-18; Luke 24:36-49; John 20:19-23; Acts 1:6-8

One day, my little boy said he would like to study the Bible once a week. In the first week he said he would like to learn how to witness. Therefore, one day while we were sitting in McDonald's. I wrote down something for my little boy to memorize. Then I told him how to share Christ with his young friends. I wrote the Bible verses and assigned him to memorize them. The next step would have been to set up a witnessing appointment with one of his friends.

He informed me that I had just told him that everyone is a sinner, and that people who die without Christ won't see Jesus. He couldn't wait to tell his friends. When he went to share his faith with his friends, they laughed at him, but he said that was all right. He just went the next morning and witnessed to other friends in the cafeteria at his school. One day he reported that his little friend Fabian had Jesus in his heart. He had accepted Christ that day in the cafeteria.

The Lord used that in my life. He told me that I couldn't ever get so cute as not to witness for Him. I can never abandon the call to the cross.

This incident reminded me of one of my favorite quotes from Dedrick Bonhoffer.[2] He made a statement that sounded so simple that it was almost insulting. He said that the only place to follow Christ is in the world. The only place to follow Christ is in the world. The eloquence of that statement is found in its implications. One cannot follow Christ in conferences. One cannot follow Christ simply in Bible studies. One doesn't follow Christ in group meetings, or simply by analyzing the issues of our time. The only place to follow Christ is in the muck, mire and the pressurized dirty details of life.

The real test of Christianity is not in our theological understanding. It is not in our ability to be sharp and impressionable. The real impact of Christianity is found in the marketplace of life. That's the only place to follow Christ. These truths are beautifully underscored in Mark 16:14-18, when Jesus tells His disciples to go out into the world and witness for Him.

This chapter deals with the challenge of making a difference in the world. It focuses on the evangelistic mission of the Black church and the context in which the church carries out its mission.

The Need for a Sense of Mission. The Black Church needs to recapture its sense of mission. That mission is the driving force of the Christian life. However, there is confusion about this mission in many churches. There is a lack of direction and a lack of mission. Often preachers quote statistics about the number of single Black women, about devastation in our community, and about the number of our people in jail. However, the question before us remains, what are we doing about these problems?

Another question is, what is God's agenda in the society in which we live? Have we allowed the industrial phase of Christianity, in a crazy backhanded way, to handcuff us and prevent us from having an impact on the world?

Has the program become the objective rather than the objective being to understand what God is doing in the world? There are three simple guideposts for recapturing a sense of mission and making a difference in the world. One is to understand the reason behind Christianity. The other is to understand the nature of one's calling. A third is to develop compassion for our ministries.

The Reason Behind Christianity. To understand the reason behind Christianity, one must understand the nature of one's mission. Mark 16:14-18 has quite a bit to say about the Christian's mission.

The mission of the Christian is related to a movement. The disciples in Mark 16 are real people with real feelings. They had gone through a range of emotions. They had left everything for the Saviour. They had abandoned businesses and had seen things fall by the wayside. They had banked their lives and futures on the Saviour. However, at the time of the event in Mark 16, they had never heard the story of the Resurrection. They had never embraced it.

In Mark 16, we see that the disciples have met at Galilee, on a mountain which Jesus had designated. The cross on which Jesus died loomed in the back of their minds. Many of the original disciples had scattered. They had turned and run. Some still doubted. Then Jesus came up and spoke to them saying, all authority has been given to Me in heaven and on earth. When they saw Him, they worshiped Him. Witness always precedes worship. Transformation always precedes communion. Then they heard of the Resurrection. Once again they had hope.

In Mark 16 they are gathered together again. They are focused on every word the Saviour is telling them. In this passage Jesus is about to tell them what it will require to change the world.

The Great Commission is not so much a geographic commission as it is a lifestyle commission. Hence, there are two purposes for every child of God. There is the vertical purpose. That is, a person is created to bring glory to God, in everything the person says and does. Then there is the horizontal purpose. That involves everything one does to fulfill his/her commission. The horizontal commission is focused on people.

The problem with most Christians in churches is that they have the wrong perspective on this whole issue. They feel that only those who are called, or involved in full-time Christian work must have this higher, elevated perspective. However, the truth is that everyone must have this perspective. Everything everyone does is a calling from God. One is just as called to work at K-Mart's as one is called to travel on an airplane or to preach.

Any place can be an arena where God calls someone to fulfill the great commission. The Christian's role in society is not to draw a paycheck from K-Mart, from the school system, or from Xerox. The Christian's role in society is to make disciples of others. That is the arena by and through which God wants the Christian to operate.

One of the reasons that Christians have difficulty with this perspective is that many are spiritual babies. They are just as carnal as they can be. They camouflage their carnality by content. That is, they know the verses. They know the statements. They know everything within their hearts, but they haven't grown. As African Americans, we must understand the nature of our commission and the nature of our calling.

The Calling. One must understand the nature of one's calling. With respect to calling, Matthew 16 has quite a bit to say. This chapter takes place at a very interesting time in our Lord's earthly ministry. At this point in time, He is riding the crest of providence and popularity. The great rejection is yet to take place. The people are still stroking Him, "hot and heavy." He still has the groupies and the hangers on. Realizing the need for

182

a focusing session or strategic retreat, He gathers His disciples together for this purpose. They have an "Urban Ministries Conference" in Caesarea Philippi.

Verse 13 says that when Jesus came into the coast of Caesarea Philippi, He asked His disciples, "Who do people say that the Son of man is?"

Really what He's doing is baiting His disciples and setting them up for Peter's revelation a few verses later. We really need to think about the question that Jesus posed. The question is, Who do people say that the Son of man is?

This passage applies both to men and women. But gender is not important here. The point is that we must learn to draw our own conclusions based on what we know, not based on what people say about us. The critical issue is not what we say about one another, but what the unsaved say about us out there in the marketplace. Whom do men say that we are? What do they say about us on the job? What do drug dealers say about us down on the corner? What are pagans all around us saying? What are non-believers saying? These questions are another way of saying, Whom do men say that I am?

In verse 14, the disciples answer that some say John the Baptist, others say Elijah, and others name Jeremiah or one of the other prophets. One can imagine Jesus folding His arms and looking at the prophetic side of things.

Then in verse 15 Jesus says, "But whom do you say that I am?" Simon Peter answers, "Thou art the Christ, the Son of the living God." Every Jew was looking for the Messiah. Every time a child was born, people would ask, "Could this be the one?" Notice what Peter has said. He said, "Thou art the Christ." The Greek translation of the Old Testament word *Maseaa* is the anointed one. Thou art the anointed one. The Son of the living God. Notice the definite article in front of "Son," symbolizing the one and only.

One can imagine Jesus turning around and staring Peter in the eyes, piercing his soul. In verse 17, Jesus says, "Blessed art thou, Simon Barjona, for flesh and blood hath not revealed it unto you." Peter may not have realized what Jesus just said. Jesus had said that this statement didn't come from a theology 101 class. One didn't get this in some intellectual discussion. This truth came from God.

Jesus wanted to remind Peter of the lowly state, the human vessel that made this divine revelation. Jesus reminds him of His name. He told Peter that Jesus was a little stone. In other words, Peter didn't need to become arrogant. God is saying here that it is important to detach ourselves from God's anointing. None of us are more than half an inch away from falling into destruction. All of us are little puddles, but He is the Rock of Ages. When God uses us, we can take the glory, but we must lay it at Jesus' feet. We can thank people when they praise us. Then we must get on our face and bless God's name.

God tells Peter that, upon this rock He will build His church. Then God says the gates of Hades shall not overpower it. The disciples knew exactly what "gates" meant. At that time, whenever an army overtook another city, they would strip the leaders naked and form a huge circle in the center of the city. They would make the leaders run around naked, in order to humiliate them. Then they would go to the gates of the city. The gates symbolized the city's strength.

The army would then remove the gates of the city from its hinges. This would symbolize that the very strength of the city had been devastated. When Jesus said that the Church would be built upon a rock, He was saying that the gates of hell would not be able to withstand the aggressive onslaught of that church.

We must not become confused, however. We are not called to an institution. We are not called to an organization. We are not called to some giant counseling center. We are called to a movement—an aggressive movement.

When the church is not mobilized, it is institutionalized. When people feel called to something that is institutional, they become institutionalized. We must be mobile. We must be pacesetters. We are to be the moral, prophetic agents in this society—not mere institutions. We must not be silent concerning the issues of our time. We just don't articulate issues. We speak to issues because we want to know how Christ relates to those issues.

A movement is a movement when it can mobilize and use resources to address needs. Once there is success, there is a tendency to preserve the gains. An example is how new churches get started. At first, the people don't have a building. They may meet in a school. At that time, they are forced to focus on people. They put their money on people. Then God blesses. All of a sudden they get into a building program. Then it all comes together. Often at that point what was a movement becomes an organization.

Outwardly there is not much difference between the movement and the organization, but there is one telltale sign. The organization is the irrational perpetuation of programs. It is like having a Sunday School convention during the second week in October, just because it was always done it that way. It is like having a preacher for a spring revival, because it was always done that way. No one stops to ask why it was done that way. A movement can go from a movement to an institution to a monument. The telltale sign of a monument is that it does nothing but reflect on the past. There is no point in remembering for remembrance's sake. The purpose for remembering is for motivation.

Compassion. Some Christians have more compassion for their ministry, their strategies, and their ideas than they do for people or for the Saviour. However, Jesus felt compassion. He was moved by people.

Matthew 9 is perhaps one of the most moving texts in the New Testament. In Matthew chapter 9, one gets a sense that Jesus is engulfed in humanity. He is healing people. He is calling people. He is confronting people. It is almost as if He does a 48-hour day in 24 hours.

Jesus is our model. We must avoid the strange brand of Christianity that does not allow for the broken, the hurt, the maimed, and the halt. Men and women need to rediscover tears. Hurting people must not be a nuisance to us. They must be our reminders of the lack of civilization among those who allow the circumstances that cause them to hurt. Sin is one big royal mess.

For example recently, in Atlanta, a woman ran out of gas in the fashionable Buckhead area. Then a man kidnapped her. While he was in the back seat raping this woman his girlfriend was driving the car. When he was finished, he allowed his cousin to take his turn. Then he took the woman over to his mother's house, to introduce her. After that, he took the woman out to a vacant, wooded area and killed her with a 12–gauge, sawed-off shotgun at point-blank range.

A local television station broadcast the man's sentencing. As the camera zoomed into the man's eyes, the judge commented on the seeming lack of remorse of this killer. It was as if the man had no soul. One couldn't help wondering where his father was. Sin is a mess, isn't it?

It Is Harvest Time. Today, most people are like sheep without a shepherd. The concept of shepherd refers to moral leadership. There is a lack of biblical, moral leadership. However, that is what is needed in our society.

It was also needed at the time of Jesus' earthly ministry. Jesus, sensing the frustration of His disciples, told them to look at the people surrounding them. He told them that the harvest is plentiful, but that the laborers were few.

Today, it is still harvest time. Christians need to begin the harvest. Christians need to reap the harvest. Tomorrow is not promised. It's harvest time, today.

BIBLE STUDY APPLICATION

Instructions: The following exercises provide the opportunity to study Mark 16:14-18; Luke 24:36-49; John 20:19-23; and

Acts 1:6-8 more closely. The first five exercises consist of five short answer "discovery" questions and a summary question. The sixth exercise provides the opportunity to apply the knowledge gained to a church-based ministry. The seventh exercise is for personal application.

"Afterward he appeared unto the eleven as they sat at meat, and upbraided them with their unbelief and hardness of heart, because they believed not them which had seen him after he was risen. And he said unto them, Go ye into all the world, and preach the gospel to every creature. He that believeth and is baptized shall be saved; but he that believeth not shall be damned. And these signs shall follow them that believe; In my name shall they cast out devils; they shall speak with new tongues; They shall take up serpents; and if they drink any deadly thing, it shall not hurt them; they shall lay hands on the sick, and they shall recover" (Mark 16:14-18).

"And as they thus spake, Jesus himself stood in the midst of them, and saith unto them, Peace be unto you. But they were terrified and affrighted, and supposed that they had seen a spirit. And he said unto them, Why are ye troubled? and why do thoughts arise in your hearts? Behold my hands and my feet, that it is I myself: handle me, and see; for a spirit hath not flesh and bones, as ye see me have. And when he had thus spoken, he showed them his hands and his feet. And while they yet believed not for joy, and wondered, he said unto them, Have ye here any meat? And they gave

him a piece of a broiled fish, and of an honeycomb. And he took it, and did eat before them. And he said unto them, These are the words which I spake unto you, while I was yet with you, that all things must be fulfilled, which were written in the law of Moses, and in the prophets, and in the psalms, concerning me. Then opened he their understanding, that they might understand the scriptures, And said unto them, Thus it is written, and thus it behooved Christ to suffer, and to rise from the dead the third day: And that repentance and remission of sins should be preached in his name among all nations, beginning at Jerusalem. And ye are witnesses of these things. And, behold, I send the promise of my Father upon you: but tarry ye in the city of Jerusalem, until ye be endued with power from on high"(Luke 24:36-49).

"Then the same day at evening, being the first day of the week, when the doors were shut where the disciples were assembled for fear of the Jews, came Jesus and stood in the midst, and said unto them, Peace be unto you. And when he had so said, he showed unto them his hands and his side. Then were the disciples glad, when they saw the Lord. Then said Jesus to them again, Peace be unto you: as my Father hath sent me, even so send I you. And when he had said this, he breathed on them, and saith unto them, Receive ye the Holy Ghost: Whosesoever sins ye remit, they are remitted unto them; and whosesoever sins ye retain, they are retained" (John 20:19-23).

188

"When they therefore were come together, they asked of him, saying, Lord, wilt thou at this time restore again the kingdom to Israel? And he said unto them, It is not for you to know the times or the seasons, which the Father hath put in his own power. But ye shall receive power, after that the Holy Ghost is come upon you: and ye shall be witnesses unto me both in Jerusalem, and in all Judaea, and in Samaria, and unto the uttermost part of the earth" (Acts 1:6-8).

1. Peter

Peter was one of the apostles who witnessed Jesus' ascension (Matthew 4:18-22). It appears that he obeyed our Lord's command.

a. What were the results of Peter's first sermon? (Acts 2)

b. Describe the circumstances surrounding Peter's first experiences with healing. (Acts 3:1-11)

c. Describe some of the environments in which Peter spread the Gospel. (Acts 4:1-21; 8:14-25; 12:1-11)

d. What is another way that Peter spread the Gospel throughout the world? (1 Peter 1:1)

e. What is yet another way that Peter spread the Gospel throughout the world? (2 Peter 1:1)

f. SUMMARY QUESTION: The Apostle Peter's influence may have been more powerful after his death than during his lifetime. Explain how this may have been the case.

2. John

John was another disciple who witnessed Jesus' ascension (Mark 1:14, 20). It appears that he obeyed Jesus' command.

a. What were the circumstances surrounding John's call to ministry? (Mark 1:19-20; Luke 4:1-11)

189

b. Who was the only disciple present at the crucifixion? (John 19:26, 27) What special assignment was he given?

c. What are some places where John preached the Gospel? (Acts 3:1-7; 4:1–4, 23-25; 8:14-17; Revelation 1:9-11)

d. What are some of the other ministries in which John was engaged? (Acts 15:6; Galatians 2:9; Revelation 1:11)

e. What are some ways that John suffered on behalf of Christ? (Acts 12:1-2; 1:9)

f. SUMMARY QUESTION: The Gospel of John, the Epistles of John and the Book of Revelation are all attributed to John, the apostle. In some ways, John's testimony may have been more powerful after his death than during his lifetime. Explain how this may have been the case.

3. Philip

Philip was among those who witnessed Jesus' ascension. It appears that he obeyed Jesus' command.

a. What was the first great evangelistic event in which Philip participated? (Acts 1:9-14; 2:1-13, 43-46)

b. What is one role that Philip played in the early church? (Acts 6:1-6)

c. What is another role that Philip played in the early church? (Acts 21:7-9)

d. What is one way that Philip carried the Gospel into the community? (Acts 8:5-13)

e. What is another way that Philip carried the Gospel into the community? (Acts 8:26-40)

f. SUMMARY QUESTION: In what sense was Philip part of a movement, as opposed to being part of a new organization?

4. Following Christ in the World

For the first century Christians, following Christ in the world meant facing the threat of violence on a daily basis.

a. Describe the circumstances surrounding the first martyr for Christ recorded in the Bible. (Acts 6:8-13; 7:59; 8:2; 22:20)

b. Describe the circumstances surrounding the death of another disciple who died for Christ. (Acts 12:2)

c. Describe the general atmosphere in which the early first century Christians carried out their ministries. (Acts 8:1-3; 9:1-2; 12:1-5)

d. In what ways was violence a part of the Apostle Paul's life? (Acts 16:13-40; 17:1-15)

e. In your opinion, did violence encourage or discourage the spread of Christianity? Explain. (Acts 8:1-8; 12:6-11)

f. SUMMARY QUESTION: Violence occurs in communities that surround African American churches today. In what ways is the violence similar to and different from the violence first century Christians faced? How should the church respond?

5. Compassion

Crawford Loritts makes the point that Christians need compassion for their ministries.

a. What difference did compassion make in the life of Moses? Whose compassion made the difference? (Exodus 2:1-10)

b. Describe one way that God has shown compassion for us. (Psalm 78:1-39)

c. Describe another way that God has shown compassion on us. (Psalm 111)

d. How did compassion affect the ministry of Christ? (Matthew 14:14; 20:34; Mark 1:41; 6:34; Luke 7:13)

e. In what ways should Christians demonstrate compassion? (1 Peter 3:8-9; 1 John 3:17–18; Jude 22—23)

f. SUMMARY QUESTION: Make a list of occupations in which Christians at your church find themselves. In what ways do they come into contact with needy people who may not have a personal, intimate relationship with the Lord? Does compassion have a place in these types of "business" relationships? Explain.

6. CHURCH–BASED MINISTRY

Select an age group. Then design a Sunday School lesson on the topic of compassion for others. What examples would you use? How would you relate the need for compassion to their daily lives?

7. PERSONAL APPLICATION

Do you have compassion for the ministry in which you are engaged? If not, ask the Lord to renew your sense of purpose and to excite you about the mission to which you are called.

CHAPTER ELEVEN

Vanessa, recent seminary graduate and a newly appointed Director of Christian Education, sat in the church library with her feet propped on a chair, looking out the window. A book she had just read was in her hand but her attention was focused elsewhere. She remembered the conversation that she had with her pastor earlier that afternoon.

"What is the mission of the African American church?" Vanessa had asked the pastor. "If I knew that, I would know how to set goals for our Christian education program."

She recalled how Pastor Sykes had smiled back at her, and how that had puzzled her.

"To tell you the truth, we never really studied Black churches in the Christian education program at the seminary," she had continued. "They told us that we needed to have mission statements, and we needed to set goals and objectives, but we never talked about the Black church."

"Okay, here's a book on the history of the Black church," Pastor Sykes had said, handing her a little red book. "Read it, and then tell me what you think the mission of the church has been in the past. We'll sit down and talk about that later today."

Suddenly Vanessa was startled out of her thoughts by the noise of sirens. Firefighters were heading toward a burning house on the next block. She got up, ran down the steps and out the door.

"The Bakers' house is on fire, and they are trying to make sure that they get all of the children out," a woman said as Vanessa walked by.

Vanessa's mind wandered back to the question she had asked Pastor Sykes. As she watched the children being evacuated from the home, she began to feel that she was about to become involved with the mission of the Black church. She couldn't wait to share her thoughts with Pastor Sykes.

The nature and mission of the African American church is certainly a controversial question, and any review of literature on it reveals a lack of consensus among ministers and laity on an answer to it. For example, in a 1986 Urban Ministries survey of 240 Black church representatives, respondents were asked to answer the question, "What is the most important mission of the Black church?" by rank ordering nine possibilities.

In first place was "worship God together as a people" (1.7), with "evangelize lost Black people" (2.7) ranking second. "Educating Black people" was tied with "healing personal and family problems" for third place (4.2). Following close behind was "developing Black leadership" (4.6). "Improving communication between Black people" (6.2), "promoting racial pride and confidence" (6.4), and "providing social services" (6.8) were in fourth, fifth and sixth places, respectively. In last place (8.3) was organizing for political action.[1]

In the article that follows, Dr. Kenneth Smith, president of Chicago Theological Seminary, addresses this controversial issue and its importance for the future of the Black church of the 21st century.

FACING THE 21ST CENTURY

Dr. Kenneth B. Smith
Matthew 16:13-19

Every 47 seconds an American child is abused or neglected. Every 67 seconds, an American teenager has a baby. Every seven minutes, an African American child is arrested for drug abuse. Every 36 minutes, an African American is arrested for drunken driving. Every 36 minutes, an African American child is killed or injured by guns. Every 53 minutes, an African American child dies because of poverty. Every school day 135,000 African American children bring some kind of weapon to school. Every day, 100,000 African American children are homeless.[2]

These statistics are overwhelming. A disproportionate share of these young people are African American. They live in Black neighborhoods and they surround Black churches. They form a part of the climate in which the Black church lives and has its being.

Very basic questions have to do with how the church defines itself, what its strengths are, what its weaknesses are, and what strategies it will use to deal with challenges it will face with the approach of the 21st century.

As we ponder these questions we are reminded of the conversation Jesus had with His disciples in Matthew 16:13-19. Jesus and His disciples had just arrived in the district of Caesarea Philippi. Jesus asked His disciples whom men said that He was.

195

They told Him that some confused Him with John the Baptist. Others confused Him with Elijah, and others confused Him with Jeremiah or one of the prophets.

When He asked their opinion, Simon Peter said that He was the Christ, the Son of the living God. Upon hearing this, Jesus informed Peter that flesh and blood had not revealed this to him, that God had revealed it to him. Jesus told him, "And I tell you, you are Peter, and on this rock I will build my church, and the powers of death shall not prevail against it" (Matthew 16:18, RSV).

In verse 18, Jesus says that it is upon the faith expressed in Peter's acknowledgment that Jesus was the Christ, the Son of the living God, that Jesus would build the Church. Moreover, the powers of death would not be able to prevail against a Church built upon such faith.

The "Black Church" was built upon such faith. It was built upon a faith which had been tested by the fires of human experience. "The powers of death" have not been able to prevail against it.

The African American church is no monolith. It is multifaceted, it grew and continues to grow out of an expression of a people of faith in the midst of their cultural and historical experiences. It is human in that it is composed of people—human beings who share a common historical Black experience in the midst of a Eurocentic climate. It is divine in that whatever structure it has, the Black Church is composed of a people who believe that God has called them into being the church. In considering what the church is today, we must consider what it has been yesterday, and we must examine what African Americans have been able to do, through the Black church.

After this historical overview, we can consider the church in the climate in which it lives today. We can explore some of the pain in the lives of people it seeks to serve. We can look at their faith and their promise. Then we can take a fresh look at the church, identifying some of its problems, some of its weak-

196

nesses, and some of its strategies for maintaining a powerful presence into the 21st century.

An examination of these topics is a tall order for a chapter of this length. Any one of these points could constitute an entire chapter. Therefore, it is only possible in the space permitted, to "wet one's appetite" by setting an agenda for clergy and laypersons. Then leaders can explore the topics at greater length and debate them in various contexts.

The Black Church of the Past. There is no question that the Black church is worthy of our celebration. It has stood a test of time. One cannot help but marvel at the development of the Black Church. It has been documented, from the lives of our forebearers that they left Africa as a people of religion, a religion native to their homeland. As they were introduced to Christianity, they fashioned it to fit their culture.

The content of their worship services, its liturgy and its style of proclamation was cultural. It was a definition of God in the world that was formed through the eyes of the ancestors. For the most part, the Black forefathers and foremothers rejected the styles of Roman Catholicism and Anglicanism and found a more fitting home among Evangelical Baptists and Methodists in the latter part of the 1700s.

Carter G. Woodson in his little book, *The History of the Negro Church,* explains, "Neither Baptist nor Methodist were at first especially interested in the Negro."[3] Woodson points out that the prominent Methodist George Whitefield of Georgia, advocated the introduction of slaves and rum for the economic improvement of the colony. Whitefield even owned slaves himself, although other Methodist leaders such as Bishops Asbury Coke and the great John Wesley opposed the institution of slavery and advocated emancipation as a first step toward evangelism.

It was out of the soil of the environment of slavery that Richard Allen and Absalom Jones emerged as the founders of the Free African Society. Soon afterward in 1794, Allen organized the independent Bethel Church, the mother church of the African Methodist Episcopal Church. This movement spread as a part of the larger independent Black Church movement. In 1822, James Varick also withdrew from the white Methodists and became the first bishop of what we now know as the African Methodist Episcopal Zion Church.

Carter G. Woodson discusses the independent Black Church movement. He notes that prior to the time when Black Methodists were organizing a structure, the Harrison Street Baptist Church was organized at Petersburg, Virginia in 1776. Harrison Street's founding was followed by a Baptist church in Williamsburg in 1785, one in Savannah in the same year, and the African Baptist church in Lexington, Kentucky in 1790.

The people founding these churches were pioneers who withdrew from white churches due to indignities they suffered in those churches and due to their desire to "Sing the songs of Zion" in their own fashion. Space does not permit further discussion of this exciting pilgrimage in early church development.

Review of the period reveals the names of powerful Black leaders who set the stage for the Black Church's struggle against slavery and for its championship for justice in later years. These leaders were, in the words of Woodson, "preachers of versatile genius." Constantly, many were engaged in a life and death struggle to free their people. They spoke fearlessly for the emancipation of the race and its elevation to citizenship. They were, on the whole, men of native talent, learning and moral strength.

Space allows for the mention of only a few of these names in addition to those already mentioned: Daniel Payne, J. W. Loguen, Charles Bennett Ray, Henry Highland Garnet, Alexander Crummell, J. W. C. Pennington, J. T. Holly, Leonard A. Grimes, Samuel R. Ward and Hiram Revels. All of these leaders served prior to the emancipation from slavery. These and others were able to create the mood for the sentiment expressed in the spiritual, "Oh freedom! Freedom over me! Before I'd be a slave, I'd be buried in my grave and go home to my Lord and be free."[4]

These leaders were the forerunners of the modern Black Church's passion for justice, political education and advocacy. It must be underscored that education was a top priority of Black Church leadership, as evidenced by the founding of Wilberforce University, which had its beginnings as early as 1847. The African Methodist Episcopal Church was the first Black church group to found a college. However, many more such colleges were founded by other denominations over the decades following.

We celebrate the faith, leadership, advocacy for justice, political activism and commitment to education of the Black church. However the Black church has done more! For millions, it has been a symbol of God's presence in their lives. It has been "The Bridge Over Troubled Waters." It has been a philanthropic community which took seriously the scriptural admonition that we are one another's keeper and that we are a place where people can hear themselves addressed and affirmed by name. Surely we celebrate the gifts and strengths of the Black church.

The Black Church Today. With this powerful image of the Black church in mind, let us now examine the climate in which this church lives today. We live in grand and awful times! We have witnessed unprecedented achievement among Black people. When I was a college student the tendency was for most students to confine their aspirations to a limited number of vocational goals such as medicine, religion, education, law and social work. That is not so today. Choices for young people entering college are more diverse today.

Like their white counterparts, Black students are flocking to programs in business administration in unprecedented numbers. Many of them have earned the coveted master's degree in business administration. Computer science is a solid choice for others. Black young people enter banking, and some even serve as commodity and stock brokers.

The natural sciences have not been beyond the horizon of today's young African Americans. For example, recently Dr. Walter Massey, of the University of Chicago, was nominated by the president to serve as the chief officer of the National Science Foundation. There have been other breakthroughs. Who could forget what the election of the late Harold Washington as mayor of Chicago meant to Black people all over this nation. He achieved this with the pivotal help of the Black church.

Another example is Douglas Wilder, a Black man who is now governor of Virginia. African Americans now preside as mayors of the cities of New York, Seattle and Washington D.C., to name just three. Recently, a Black man, Harvey Gant, former two-term mayor of Charlotte, North Carolina challenged the infamous Senator Jesse Helms for the U.S. Senate seat. It was a close vote.

Moreover, one cannot underestimate the power of the presence of the Reverend Jesse Jackson as a serious presidential candidate in the Democratic Party. Today, a Black man is chairman of the Joint Chiefs of Staff. Even though there remains only one Black person on the Supreme Court, and only one in the President's Cabinet, these are achievements. Yes! John H. Johnson calls this "Succeeding Against the Odds," which is the title of his autobiography.[5]

The Black church has been involved in most of the struggles that led to these achievements. The Black church began achieving such victories prior to emancipation. It was no coincidence that the late Dr. Martin Luther King, Jr. was "The Reverend Dr. King," a son of this same African American Church. His impact was both national and worldwide. He inspired a whole generation of African Americans to break down the doors of oppression and take their places among free men and women. He encouraged them to be free, not only on buses and at lunch counters, but in voting booths, and in every other place where their aspirations took them.

Bart Landry in his book, *The New Black Middle Class,* tells us that the Black middle class is still growing, but grew at a slower rate in the 1970s, 1980s and 1990s. "Between 1960 and 1970, The Black middle class doubled in size, achieving a growth rate of 106.8 percent. Between 1970 and 1980, its rate of growth declined to 61.9 percent. Whites experienced just the opposite [pattern of growth]. Their middle class increased faster in the 1970s than in the 1960s."[6]

The decline in the Black middle class growth rate, Landry points out, was due in large part to Blacks' greater vulnerability to economic slowdown. Recall that the times are both grand and awful! It has often been said that when the nation suffers a recession, it is a depression in the Black community.

William Julius Wilson in *The Truly Disadvantaged* writes: "The social problems of urban life in the United States are, in large measure, the problems of racial inequality. The rates of crime, drug addiction, out-of-wedlock births, female-headed families, and welfare dependency have risen dramatically in the last several years, and they reflect a noticeably uneven distribution by race."[7] While there has been some progress there are immense problems facing African Americans and the problems are rooted in race—problems that are supported by both public and private policy.

The disproportionate involvement of Blacks in violent crime is clearly revealed in the statistics on city arrests. Wilson notes that Blacks constitute 13 percent of the population of cities, but they account for over half of all city arrests for violent crimes. In Chicago, for example, as in other major urban centers, Blacks are not only more likely to commit murder, but they are also more likely to be the victims of murder.

Wilson discusses family disintegration, welfare dependency and economic hardships. There is no doubt that contemporary racial discrimination has contributed to or aggravated the social and economic problems of millions of Black people. What is happening to African American families mirrors what is happening to millions of children, especially young Black males whom Andrew Billingsley describes as "an endangered species."[8]

We've all heard the recent reports on Black men. In an October 15 article in the *Chicago Tribune,* the writer quotes from a report by The Sentencing Project based in Washington, D.C.:

"One in every four young Black men between the ages of 20 and 29 is under the control of the correction system, increasingly because of drug convictions. Drug use cuts across racial lines, but drug enforcement focuses on the inner cities and Blacks."[9]

The conditions of so many of our people challenge not only the church, but every other Black group, agency and institution in the community. This means that the very existence of the race is at stake. Increasingly, we are facing people with a declining faith in God, faith in themselves and faith in the future. There is a pervasive sense of hopelessness. The people of God can hear the cry of the Psalmist: "How long wilt thou forget me, O Lord?" (Psalm 13:1)

The pain is so great that many turn to substance abuse to dull it. The condition has been explained as pathological, but people who describe it theologically, quote Scriptures such as the following:

"The sins of the fathers and mothers are indeed visited upon unborn generations" (Numbers 14:18, NKJV).

"And even if the gospel is veiled, it is veiled only to those who are perishing. In their case the God of this world has blinded the minds of unbelievers to keep them from seeing the light of the gospel of the glory of Christ who is the likeness of God" (2 Corinthians 4:3-4).

The Black Church of the Future. The Black Church must be equal to the tasks before it. It can serve people in spite of the climate of the times. It has always been resilient and has been able to adjust to the demands placed before it.

Let us begin with the leadership, particularly the clergy leadership. There is a loosening of moral fiber among Black leadership. However, leaders must be persons of moral integrity, to conduct the war to save our people. There can be no more practice of the principle of "Do as I say and not what I do." Leaders cannot preach one thing and then act contrary to their own sermons. There is no substitute for being clean in body, mind and spirit. We must keep in mind that God called leaders to be servants and not masters. Leaders must be honest with the people for whom they have been called to care.

Leaders must move beyond the simple view of the church's mission and deal with all of the problems which are destroying Black people. The Gospel speaks to the whole person—the body, the mind and the spirit. For example, this means that leaders must become knowledgeable about public policy because public policy determines the budgets and it determines programs that could help or hurt African Americans. Leaders must be advocates for the people.

Leaders must move beyond artificial theological and biblical barriers which cause them to reject others who are genuinely called to be servants. The Church and its leadership require the best minds and hearts for the work of ministry.

Leaders must form ecumenical relationships. God does not see His children in terms of whether they are Baptist, Methodist, Presbyterian or Pentecostal. God looks upon His children in terms of whether they are faithful to His Word and whether they hear the cries of needy people and whether they are willing to serve them.

Leaders must also network with others in our communities who work toward uplifting African Americans. Leaders must form these networks with other institutions and other professionals. The process begins with dialogue.

Leaders must encourage young, informed leadership to enter the political life of the community. Such people need to be nurtured and supported. Leaders must train African Americans to recognize and resist against those who do wrong and harm. Leaders must be informed, for God's sake! Preaching without substance is blasphemy. Without sound preaching and sound teaching, how will the people know right from wrong?

In the new century, the Black church's strength and presence will depend upon its leadership's capacity to be caregivers. The church must be a drum major for justice, and an advocate for the "least of these" among us. The Black church's strength and presence will also depend upon the capacity of the church to be a place where people feel empowered to discuss all community issues, explore all of the community's pain and then fashion a promise for the community.

Its strength and presence will depend upon its capacity to develop educational programs for young people and adults alike which focus on heritage, self-affirmation, human sexuality, what it means to be a man or woman, health, and biblical principles.

The Black church's strengths and presence will depend upon whether the army of volunteers housed in every church will be able to move beyond individual religious approaches to a communal religious response. This means moving from bench membership to embracing young men and women and becoming role models and mentors for them. How will children know if someone does not show them? If not now, when? If not us, who?

Conclusion. In conclusion, I never cease to be inspired by the words of that patron saint of our people, the late Benjamin E. Mays, who, for more than two decades was president of Morehouse College in Atlanta, Georgia. He said, "It must be born in mind that the tragedy of life does not lie in not reaching your goal. The tragedy lies in having no goal to reach. It isn't a calamity to die with dreams unfulfilled, but it is a calamity not to dream. It is not a disaster to be unable to capture your ideal, but it is a disaster to have no ideal to capture. It is not a disgrace to have no stars to reach for. Not failure, but low aim, is sin."[10]

As members of the African Americans church we must make certain that we aim high. As agents of God, we must enable the church to aim high and broad as we approach the 21st century, with purpose.

BIBLE STUDY APPLICATION

Instructions: The following exercises provide the opportunity to study Matthew 16:13-19 more closely. The first five exercises consist of discovery questions, followed by a summary question. The sixth exercise provides the opportunity to apply wisdom gained from the exercises and from the chapter to the development of a church-based ministry. The seventh exercise provides for personal application.

> *"When Jesus came into the coasts of Caesarea Philippi, he asked his disciples, saying, Whom do men say that I the Son of man am? And they said, Some say that thou art John the Baptist: some, Elias; and others, Jeremias, or one of the prophets. He saith unto them, But whom say ye that I am? And Simon Peter answered and said, Thou art the Christ, the Son of the living God. And Jesus answered and said unto him, Blessed art thou, Simon Bar-jona: for flesh and blood hath not revealed it unto thee, but my Father which is in heaven. And I say also unto thee, That thou art Peter, and upon this rock I will build my church; and the gates of hell shall not prevail against it. And I will give unto thee the keys of the kingdom of heaven: and whatsoever thou shalt bind on earth shall be bound in heaven: and whatsoever thou shalt loose on earth shall be loosed in heaven" (Matthew 16:13-19).*

1. The Climate of the Times

Jesus carried out His earthly ministry among a group of people suffering from a history of defeats.

a. What had happened to the original Jewish state, consisting of twelve tribes? (2 Chronicles 10:1—11:17)

b. What had happened to both the Northern and the Southern Kingdoms that had resulted from the split in the Jewish state? (2 Kings 17:1-23; 25:1-21)

c. What events had resulted in the Jews returning to Jerusalem and rebuilding the temple? (2 Chronicles 36:22, 23; Ezra 1:2, 3)

d. Between the close of the Old Testament and the opening of the New Testament, Alexander the Greek and his descendants conquered and ruled Palestine (336-323 B.C.). Then the Seleucid kings of Syria conquered Palestine (about 200 B.C.). Afterwards there was a revolt of the Jewish Maccabees which restored Israel's independence (142 B.C.). Later, a civil war in Israel led to Rome's domination (63 B.C.). Who was the Roman emperor ruling at the time of Christ? (Matthew 1:5; Luke 2:1) Who was the monarch appointed by Rome to rule Palestine? (Matthew 2:1; Luke 1:5)

e. How were the Jews treated under the Caesars and Herod? (Luke 2:1-7; Matthew 2:1-23)   Had the Jewish religion been wiped out, due to their defeats? (Luke 2:22-43)

f. SUMMARY QUESTION: Considering your answers to a-e, discuss the resilience (power to "come back") of the Jewish religion. Draw parallels between the resiliency of the Jewish religion and the resiliency of the Black church. Does Dr. Smith's article provide further insights about this?

2. Hopes for a Messiah

The Jews had many conflicting expectations for a Messiah. This affected how they saw Christ.

a. What are some of the stated expectations that people had of Jesus? (Luke 24:13-24; John 6:1-2, 8-15; Acts 1:6-7)

b. Why might some people have confused Jesus with Elias

(the Greek form of Elijah) the prophet? (1 Kings 17:8-24; 18:1-2, 20-39; 2 Kings 2:1-12; Luke 9:1-9; Malachi 4:5-6)

c. Why might some people have confused Jesus with John the Baptist? (Isaiah 40:3-5; Malachi 3:1; Matthew 3:1; 14:1-12; Mark 1:1-4)

d. How might Jesus' lifestyle have been the source of confusion as to whether He was one of the prophets? (Deuteronomy 18:16-19; 1 Kings 14:1-3; 2 Kings 4:1, 38, 42; 6:1-7; Luke 9:57-58)

e. What had Jesus already told people that He had come to do? (Luke 4:16-25)

f. SUMMARY QUESTION: What was the basic confusion of the Jews over the role that Jesus was to play? Compare and contrast their confusion with the confusion many people have today over the role of the Black church in the community. What light does Dr. Smith's article shed on this controversial issue?

3. The Son of Man

Our Lord refers to Himself as the Son of man more than eighty times in the New Testament. This phrase suggests something about His understanding of the role He would play.

a. How did Jesus become both the Son of man and the Son of God? (Isaiah 7:14; John 1:1-16; Matthew 1:11-17; 18:24; Romans 8:3)

b. What similarities and differences were there between Jesus and Ezekiel, the only other person referenced as a Son of man, in Scripture? (Ezekiel 2:1-7; 4:1-5)

c. Draw a meaning of the term, "Son of man" from some of the contexts in which Jesus uses it. (Matthew 11:16-19; 20:26-28; Luke 9:57-58)

d. What are some other contexts in which Jesus uses the term, "Son of man"? (Luke 12:40; 19:10; Matthew 12:40; 20:18; 26:2; 24:37-44)

e. There were many prophecies concerning the Son of man. What were some of them? (Psalm 22:1, 2, 6; Matthew 27:39-46)

f. SUMMARY QUESTION: Compare and contrast the role of the African American church in the African American community with the role that Jesus, the Son of man, played.

4. Son of God

Throughout the New Testament, Jesus is also referenced as the Son of God.

a. In what sense did Jesus as God's Son, pre-date His existence in Palestine? (John 8:58; 17:5; Romans 8:3; 2 Corinthians 8:8-9)

b. What evidence is there that Jesus considered Himself as the Son of God? (John 15:8-10; Matthew 3:4-17)

c. Draw some meanings of the term, "Son of God," from some contexts in which it is used. (John 5:21, 23; 14:1)

d. Was Peter the only one who realized that Jesus was the "Son of God"? (Matthew 4:1-3; 8:28-29; John 1:34; 20:28, 31)

e. How do human beings become sons and daughters of God? (John 1:12; Romans 8:14; Philippians 2:15; 1 John 3:1; 3:2)

f. SUMMARY QUESTION: In what sense are African American Christians sons and daughters of God? What does this say about the powerful role that they play in the world?

5. The Rock

Jesus told Peter that the church would be built upon the foundation that Jesus was the Son of God. He said the gates of hell would not be able to prevail against it.

a. What is one way that the Lord is our Rock? (2 Samuel 22:1-3; Psalm 18:1-2; 62:7)

b. What is another way in which God is our Rock? (Deuteronomy 32:15; Exodus 17:6)

c. How is Christ our Rock? (John 4:7-15; Exodus 17:6; 1 Corinthians 10:4)

d. In what sense is Christ the Rock upon which the spiritual Church is built? (Ephesians 2:19-22; Romans 9:32; 1 Corinthians 1:23-24)

e. What are some images of rocks in Scripture? (Exodus 17:6; 33:19-23; Numbers 20:7-9; Deuteronomy 32:10-13)

f. SUMMARY QUESTION: In what sense is the African American church a rock in the African American community? In what sense is it a rock in the world?

6. CHURCH–BASED MINISTRY

Based on the information gained from exercises 1-5, write a mission statement for your local church. In your mission statement, state the goal your church can have within the context of the 21st century. How will it serve in the capacity of Son of man, Son of God, and Rock? Then write a mission statement for the auxiliary to which you belong.

7. PERSONAL APPLICATION

What is your role in your family, church and community? Do you reflect attributes of being a son or daughter of God, a rock, a son of man? How can you go about fine-tuning your image? Where will you get the power?

CHAPTER TWELVE

It was 1:00 in the afternoon. It was hot and flies were swarming throughout the village, as usual. Annu stared through the door of the home in which he lived, down the road from a nearby relief station. About an hour ago, he and his mother had their noonday prayers. He lived in a small home, in a small Ethiopian village. The walls of his home were made of wood, cemented by mud. The ceiling was made mostly of straw. There was no air conditioning and no screens to keep the flies out.

During the last two weeks, Annu's best friend Diala and Annu's sister had both died of illnesses related to malnutrition. They were two of at least 50 people who had died during the past month.

Thousands of miles away, across the Atlantic Ocean, in New York City, the Joneses sat in their high-rise, air conditioned apartment, watching an evening talk show while eating dinner. The host had invited representatives of the major news networks as guests and was asking them why the crisis in Ethiopia and in other African nations was not being covered.

One of the network executives responded, "We cover issues in which Americans express interest. They aren't too interested in hearing about hunger and famine. It doesn't have top priority among daily news items."

> *Mrs. Jones was horrified. "Not interested?" she said to her husband. "I thought that this was supposed to be a Christian country!"*

Dr. John Henrik Clarke, in "African World Revolution," cites various estimates of the numbers of people of African descent living throughout the world. Based on his projections, in Africa there are well in excess of the 500 million people which the census has reported as though there hasn't been any growth for decades. Another estimated 100 million Asian "untouchables" are of African descent. In the Americas, Caribbean region and South America, there are another estimated 200 million people of African descent.

Clarke notes that, regardless of locale, Black people throughout the Diaspora and Africa are suffering from various combinations of famine, poverty, political oppression and racism. Most of these conditions are not reported on any regular basis by the Eurocentric press of the "New World Order."

These conditions are also not reported within African American churches on any regular basis. Moreover, results of surveys of Black church representatives do not reflect many ongoing outreach or educational programs that make people aware of these problems, or that involve them in trying to solve them. For example, in 1991, Eric Lincoln asked 2,150 Black churches to list their most important internal organizations and auxiliaries. Missionary societies or outreach programs did not make the list of the top nine.[1]

In a similar study, Colleen Birchett distributed questionnaires to 240 church representatives, asking them to rank various missions of the Black church in terms of importance.

The social services mission was ranked #8 out of a possible nine, and organizing for political action was ranked as #9.[2]

These statistics paint a grim picture. However, in the following article, Dr. Iva Carruthers says that there is hope—if Africans throughout the Diaspora will become hearers and doers of the Word of God.

SOWING SEEDS IN THE DIASPORA

Dr. Iva Carruthers
Matthew 13:4-9, 18-23

The Parable of the Sower in Matthew 13 provides both a visual and spiritual context which helps to explain challenges facing people of African descent at the end of the 21st century. The African Diaspora refers to the separation and presence of African people away from their homeland, Africa.

The message of this chapter concerning the challenges facing Africans in the Diaspora is not meant to be entertaining. It is very serious. People of African descent must develop a very serious agenda for the 21st century. It is the purpose of this chapter to elevate the reader and the author to empowering visions echoed in the words of our forefathers and foremothers and in the Word of God.

Today, more than ever, empowering visions are needed because for Africans of the Diaspora, the prophetic echoes of our ancestors are quickly being realized. These echoes are the drumbeats whose calls are pronouncing that as we enter the next millennium, Africans of the Diaspora are at the crossroads—the crossroads which lead us either to victory or to becoming a "lost tribe" of the world. It is a crossroad which will prove us to be either sowers of good fruit or sowers of chaff.

One can melt (or blend) the sociological to the Christological for guidance, in reflecting on African communities outside of continental Africa. This is so because of the commonalities shared by African communities whether in the Asian Pacific, throughout the Americas, in India among Dravidian people, in Europe or throughout the Caribbean.

The book entitled *African Presence in the Americas,* edited by Shawna Moore, represents an interdisciplinary approach to this topic. It is a compilation of papers presented at the 1987 Conference of Negritude, Race and Ethnicity in the Americas.[3] This chapter will make references to this great work, as it provides the backdrop for this examination of the African Diaspora both from an Afrocentric and from a Christological point of view. The chapter will attempt to identify prospects for the future, based on an examination of the past.

Three major topics will be addressed: 1) portraits of Blacks of the Diaspora; 2) an Afrocentric and Christological understanding of our condition; and 3) some echoes of our ancestors.

A Snapshot Portrait of Blacks of the Diaspora. If we were assembling an African family album of the world, we would discover that Africans of the Diaspora represent 400 million people with ancestral and cultural ties to another 640 million people on the continent of Africa. That is more than one billion African people who share the recent 500-year experience of oppression by white supremacy and racism.

This 500-year history has affected the lives of African Americans in every respect: economically, socially, psychologically and even sexually. The commonality of culture among these African people has defied time, space and circumstance, so that there are still evidences of family, spiritual, linguistic, and communal similarities between them. To recognize these similarities, one must consider Africans of the Diaspora—before and after the 500–year period of the holocaust of slavery.

The Pre-Classical Period. Beginning with the Pre-Classical Period, prior to 300,000 B.C., Blacks are seen crossing the Bering

SOWING SEEDS IN THE DIASPORA

Strait. One sees Black Australoids, Black Pygmynoids, Black Dravidians, Black Melaesoids, Black Hamites, and Black Negritoids. The tools which these people created have been found matching those of the Orange Free State in southern Africa. Both sets of tools can be carbon-dated from 29,000 B.C. to 20,000 B.C. Statuettes found in Ecuador dating from 13,000 B.C. to 8,000 B.C., prove Blacks were there during that early period. Africanoid dolicephalic skulls from that same period have been found in Brazil, Ecuador, Chile and the Andes. The features of Zapata Heads that are 10 feet tall and weigh 10-20 tons, prove that Blacks were present in 2000 B.C. among the Mayans in the Veracruz area of Mexico.

There is also evidence that Blacks were present in the high sea voyages of the Phoenicians, the Carthagenians and Ethiopians, in 600 B.C. Blacks were present in 1305-07 A.D., when King Abubakari II sailed his great armada of 400 ships on the Atlantic Ocean, and while Mansa Musa, his brother, ruled the great Mali Kingdom.

A More Contemporary Snapshot. The Garifunas of Honduras identify themselves as the only non-enslaved Black group in the Americas, perhaps even in the world. In 1589 Spanish priests recorded the presence of free Blacks in the Esmeraldas area of Ecuador. In 1780 18,000 slaves were reported in Ecuador. Primarily they came from Zaire, Angola and Rwanda. There are twice as many Blacks in Brazil (60 million)as there are in the United States (30 million). Moreover, the Black matron saint of Catholicism is revered by both white and Black Brazilians. The Matron Saint of Costa Rica is also a Black woman, called "Our Lady of the Angels." And in 1987 President Oscar Arias Sanchez of Costa Rica accepted the Nobel Peace Prize in declaration and on behalf of his Nubian/Black blood. Just as Blacks in Cuba gave impetus and victory to the Cuban revolution, only to be shunned by the white Cuban leadership which later came to power, so has been the experience in the Sandanista revolution of Nicaragua.

Africans of the Asian world are totally invisible and under-counted. However, evidences of trade between Africa and China date back to 2000 B.C. The Dravidians of India, now referred to as the "untouchables," were the indigenous Africans of India before the white/Aryan invasion of their land around 700 B.C. The African–looking Montagnard people of Vietnam certainly saw a mirror reflection of themselves among the Black soldiers who fought in that war against them. Today's Melanesian, Polynesian, and Micronesian Africans are in a struggle against the forces and institutions of white colonial masters. This struggle reflects the continuity of the African presence in Asia.

Africans in Europe represent yet another part of this great African family album. African history in Europe is significantly marked by the victories of General Hannibal (247-183 B.C.) against the Roman Empire and the Moors' dominance and presence in Spain from 700 A.D. through the 15th century. The Africans which the European world found in Peru in 1527 were direct descendants of the Moors who conquered Spain. Most recently, second through fourth generation immigrants to Europe from the West Indies find themselves suddenly confronting a New World order. The 1992 European Confederation and im-migration policy is proving to be discriminatory, oppressive and insidious. The status of immigration in Europe is now under a secretariat charged with addressing the problems of illegal drug trafficking, AIDS, hostages and immigration. The very combina-tion of these issues illustrated the degree to which Europeans feel that the presence of Black and dark-skinned peoples threatens the health and welfare of Pan-European unity.

A Christological Perspective. With that family album portrait and sociological description of Africans, a Christological comment is needed. Christology is the study of the doctrines of Christ. When we study the Diaspora from Christ's viewpoint, we seek to uncover the wisdom that Christ provides concerning Africans throughout the world. The divine Word always provides deeper insight and understanding.

216

From a Christological perspective, the definition of the term Diaspora means "that which is sown." It means much more than the scattering of a people from their homeland throughout the world. It refers to that which is to be sown for the purpose of spiritual growth. The scattering is for the purpose of setting something in motion, or spreading it abroad. Thus, from a Christological perspective, the Diaspora refers to an intentional scattering to set something in motion.

Indeed, Black people have been scattered. However, many Black people hesitate to claim ownership of the divine responsibility of being sowers in the biblical sense of "Diaspora." Thus, as Africans enter the next millennium, Africans of the Diaspora are at a crossroads with a crisis in leadership understanding, specifically impacting the Christian community. Leaders lack sufficient understanding of the fundamental relationship between our history, i.e., the African world experience, and the imperatives of our faith, the Christian covenant with God. Both of these aspects of African identity carry fundamental imperatives.

Some Black people have heard the Word, but too few are doers of the Word. For example, the last 30 years have evidenced little institutional development and less institutional sustainment of our communities. Our leadership has been lured by the promises of integration and inclusion. At this moment in time, at this crossroads, the wisdom of African ancestors has been held more in the bosom of the masses than in the minds and actions of the privileged leaders, the disciples and apostles of Black freedom.

The result is that, as we enter the third millennium, beginning in the year 2000 AD, leaders of the Diaspora need to be reminded and held accountable to the Parable of the Sower. Too many Black people have been, in Jesus' words, "devoured by outsiders." Black leaders have been characterized more by the African proverb which tells of two birds who were arguing and a third which came and devoured them. One needs only to examine the politics of Chicago's last mayoral election and the recent Clarence Thomas hearings for examples of this.

217

In Jesus' words, too many of us have "lacked deepness of earth" (Matthew 13:5). This is evidenced by nation-states where the foundation of peoplehood has been driven more by political expediency and by the expediency of gaining individual favors from the Super Powers than by expediency of a more longterm agenda for intra–country planning. The current state of affairs of the Federation of West Indies is an example of this.

In Jesus' words, indeed we have "lacked deepness of roots," resulting in leaders who have bought into an illusion of racial democracy where color and class matter, but race doesn't. An examples of this is Brazil, with its 60 million Blacks and 132 different names for color. Another example is the United States, where leaders use the Black agenda as their occupational career ladder, subject to immediate compromise at the next promotional offering.

It is reported by the watchtower of the African Diaspora that the seeds being sown in Black communities are seeds of self-destructive consumerism, drugs and immediate gratification. They are seeds of abandonment of the land, rejection of traditions, rejection of history, and foregoing of institutional development, for mainstream integration and inclusion. These seeds have not brought forth new fruit 100-fold, 60-fold, or even 30-fold. Rather, these seeds have yielded only several generations of chaff, disconnected from the past, and absorbed by the glitter and glamour of high speed video, the inertia of drugs, the quest for individuality, indifference and the "Clarence Thomases" and their "uppitiness" in the New World order.

These are the seeds which betray the sowers of our past and the sowers of the Word. More than ever as we approach the year 2000, the echoes of our ancestors are reverberating. They are reverberating on the heels of the Thomas hearings, which were probably the most devastating media event of Africans of the world since D.W. Griffith's shamelessly racist movie "Birth of a Nation."

Black people must be historically astute. The 500th year celebration of the Columbus voyage was much more than an acknowledgment and affirmation of the "discovery" of the New

World. It was also an historical watershed to usher in the New World Order for the next millennium.

In 1492 Columbus sailed the ocean blue and up "popped" the New World. In 1992, the Confederation of European nations, in compliance with Bush's New World Order, has organized European western white unity for the next millennium. Like Lincoln's Emancipation Proclamation, with the goal of unity above all else, the 1992 Pan European Unity Act called for a cease fire on the "communism versus capitalism" debate, the "American versus European" debate and the European ethnic debates. Instead, it elevated the vested interest of Pan European unity, at all cost.

This New World Order in 12 months has realigned the white world hegemony or power as the walls of Communism came tumbling down while the wall forbidding African world immigration was being emphatically erected. Black author Chester Himes, in one of his classic works, noted what the masses have always known: "...a Communist ain't nothing anyway but a broke capitalist: white all the same."[4]

In the past 12 months, this Pan European unity has set forth in the Middle East U.S. military bases of operations in Kuwait and Israel, a country which gets more of the United States tax dollar than all 51 countries of Africa combined. By now Israel has restructured its tentacles into Africa through a "front door" policy with South Africa.

In three days of salaciously sensational television at its finest, this same Pan European unity reawakened and shook ajar, lest some forget, the stereotypic images of the bestiality, sexual prowess, and demon-possession attributed to the Black male. Clarence Thomas was cast in the starring role, and his victimized, sex-starved, Black female co-star in this media event was Anita Hill. The Europeans did this while making clear the new criteria and rules through which Blacks, or at least the exceptional ones among us, can enter the gates of this New World order. Clarence Thomas, notwithstanding his white wife, is an example of this.

219

The longterm impact of this media event not only put "Birth of a Nation" to shame, but also distracted attention from the concomitant veto of the unemployment benefits extension bill, the beginning of the annual lottery to ensure citizenship for people of European ancestry (especially the Irish), and a $500 million subsidy (of U.S. tax dollars) to the Russian economy.

Considering these realities, Blacks of the Diaspora must be blessed with "eyes that see and ears that hear," Black people must be "doers of the Word" in ways that bring forth new life and hope for African people of the world. Not to do so will surely result in the reality of becoming the forgotten tribes of Africa during the next millennium.

For as hard as it may be to imagine, think a moment about the possibility of a New World Order in which some people are present who are Black, but there is no presence of Black African peoplehood. Imagine a people without a race. A few may remain, and be included in the mainstream of society, but the masses decimated by drugs, AIDS, starvation and population transfer would not be seen by civilized eyes again. This is where Black people are headed, and whether Black people get there will depend entirely on Blacks of this generation. It will depend on whether Blacks of this generation have visions and aspirations.

Proverbs 29:18 says, "Where there is no vision, the people perish: but he that keepeth the law, happy is he" (King James Version). The Living Bible translation of this proverb says, "Where there is ignorance of God, the people run wild; but what a wonderful thing it is for a nation to know and keep its laws!"

The Echoes of the Ancestors. There are lessons to be learned, symbolized by the mythical bird of Ghana, the Sankofa Bird, and echoed by our ancestors. These lessons guide the concluding remarks. The "Sankofa Bird" represents the trinity of existence and praxis. It is referenced as the transubstantiation of life. It is the harmony between 1) matter and spirit; 2) theory and practice; and 3) birth and death.

This African bird image, with the beak touching the tail, reflects the quest and recovery of past knowledge, in order to direct the future. Similarly, the echo of Henry McNeal Turner of the AME Church, in one of his sermons of the 1890s, challenges African people to dare to see God as themselves and to respect Black people.

> "Every race of people since time began who have attempted to describe their god by words, or by paintings, or by carvings, or by any other form or figure, have conveyed the idea that the God who made them and shaped their destinies was symbolized in themselves, and why should not the Negro believe that he resembles God as much so as other people? We do not believe that there is any hope for a race of people who do not believe that they look like God...We are no stickler as to God's color, anyway, but if He has any...we certainly protest against God being a white man or against God being white at all...We conclude these remarks by repeating...God is a Negro."[5]

Then there are the echoes of Edward Wilmot Blyden, Mary McLeod Bethune, Carter G. Woodson, and Alexander Crummell. The echo of Edward Wilmot Blyden chides us for not realizing that our linkages to continental Africa are intricately wedded to survival in the Diaspora:

> "We need some African Power, some great center of the race where our physical, pecuniary, and intellectual strength may be collected. We need some spot where such an influence may go forth in behalf of the race as shall be felt by the nations. We are now so scattered and divided that we can do nothing...so long as we remain thus divided, we may expect imposi-

tion...an African nationality is our great need...we must build up Negro States we must establish and maintain the various institutions."[6]

The echo of Mary McLeod Bethune, builder of institutions, whose love of elephants and diligent, prayerful life symbolizes the African remembrances rooted in deep spirituality, reminds Africans that it is faith in God and in themselves which will protect them:

"Sometimes as I sit communing in my study I feel that death is not far off...Death neither alarms nor frightens one who has had a long career of fruitful toil...So, as my life draws to a close, I will pass them on to Negroes everywhere in the hope that an old woman's philosophy may give them inspiration. Here, then is my legacy...I leave you faith. Faith is the first factor in life devoted to service. Without faith nothing is possible. With it, nothing is impossible. Faith in God is the greatest power, but great too, is faith in one's self...I leave you dignity...I leave you, finally, a responsibility to our people...Our children must never lose their zeal for building a better world."[7]

The echo of Carter G. Woodson is an admonition that the creative genius of the African mind has been in suspension during this period of African diasporic suppression, because the educated are so busy emulating the white way:

"When a Negro has finished his education in our school, then, he has been equipped to begin the life of an Americanized or Europeanized white man, but before he steps from the threshold of his alma mater he is told by his teachers...that he must go back to his own people from whom he has been estranged by a vision of ideals which in his disillusionment he will realize that he cannot attain...In this effort to imitate...to conform quickly to the standard of the whites and thus remove the pretext for the barriers between the races...You simply have a larger number of persons doing what others have been doing. The unusual gifts of the race have not thereby been developed, and an unwilling world, therefore, continues to wonder what the Negro is good for."[8]

And lastly the echo of Alexander Crummell, Episcopal minister speaking in 1875, says that Black people have a divine responsibility or God will surely forsake them:

"The great general laws of growth and superiority are unchangeable. The Almighty neither relaxes nor alters them for the convenience of any people. Conformity, then, to this demand for combination of forces is a necessity which we, as a people, cannot resist without loss and ruin...The special duty before us is to strive for footing and for superiority in this land, on the line for [our] race...For if we do not look after our own interest, as a people, and strive for [our] advantage, no other people will. It is folly for mere idealists to content themselves with the notion that 'we are American citizens'; that, 'as American citizens, ours is the common heritage and destiny of the nation'; that there is but one tide in this land; and we shall flow with all others on it. ...What this race needs in the country is power...and that comes from character, and character is the product of religion, intelligence, virtue, family order, superiority, wealth, and the show of industrial forces...The very first effort of the colored people should be to lay hold of them; and then they will take such root in this American soil that

only the convulsive upheaving of the judgment-day
can throw them out!"[9]

Today Africans throughout the Diaspora must ask themselves, as Toni Cade Bambara did, "What are we pretending we have forgotten?"[10] Those of us with "ears that hear" and "eyes to see" must look at Africans of the Diaspora, and at the rich, opportunistic responsibility to the ancestral land of ourselves and of God. What is preventing Blacks as a people from believing that they can again set something in motion, believing that once again there is a higher calling and a destiny on the world stage?

Perhaps, people of the African Diaspora, more than any other people of the world, have an understanding of the vision for the kingdom of God on earth. Black people have this vision, if they dare to stop pretending that they have forgotten.

Those who believe in the divine harmony of African and Christian selves are called upon to turn the Church back to being doers of the Word. The Black Church experience of the Americas has traditionally made its mark and sown its seeds through active ministries of mutual aid for, by and through themselves.

Summary. Truly, Black people are at a divine and prophetic crossroads, a crossroads predicted by God. If the reader believes this, the reader will not leave this chapter without an agreement to take one specific action of sacrifice, in collective concert, subordinate to his/her individual self and associations, and to support one institution, one organization or one leadership agenda or delegated team. The reader must prove to him/herself what power a few in the African Diaspora can have in one span of one committed moment. That one moment can help us to envision the unused power we hold. Too many of our seeds have become chaff and not fruit, and time is running out. I end this chapter with the words of Alexander Crummell, spoken in 1882: "And therefore I close, as I began, with the admonitory tones of the text. God grant they may be heeded at least by you, who form this congregation, in your sacred work here, and in all your other relations."[11]

BIBLE STUDY APPLICATION

Instructions: The following exercises provide the opportunity to study the Parable of the Sower in Matthew 13:4-9, 18-23 more closely. The first five exercises consist of a series of short answer questions followed by a summary question. The sixth exercise provides the opportunity to apply principles from this chapter to a church–based ministry. The seventh exercise is for personal application.

"And when he sowed, some seeds fell by the way side, and the fowls came and devoured them up: Some fell upon stony places, where they had not much earth: and forthwith they sprung up, because they had no deepness of earth: And when the sun was up, they were scorched; and because they had no root, they withered away. And some fell among thorns; and the thorns sprung up, and choked them: But other fell into good ground, and brought forth fruit, some an hundredfold, some sixtyfold, some thirtyfold. Who hath ears to hear, let him hear.

Hear ye therefore the parable of the sower. When any one heareth the word of the kingdom, and understandeth it not, then cometh the wicked one, and catcheth away that which was sown in his heart. This is he which received seed by the way side. But he that received the seed into stony places, the same is he that heareth the word, and anon with joy receiveth it; Yet hath he not root in himself, but dureth for a while: for when tribulation or persecution ariseth because of the word, by and by he is offended. He also that received seed among the thorns is he that heareth the word; and the care of this world, and the deceitfulness of riches, choke the word, and he becometh unfruitful. But he that received seed into the good ground is he that heareth the word, and understandeth it; which also beareth fruit, and bringeth forth, some an hundredfold, some sixty, some thirty" (Matthew 13:4-9, 18-23).

1. The Sower

Many praise songs, parables and prophecies make use of the image of the sower to teach important spiritual truths.

a. In what ways can the sowers in Isaiah 28:22-29 be compared to Christians working in the African American community today?

b. In what ways can Psalm 107 be applied to Black people throughout the Diaspora?

c. In what ways can Psalm 126 be applied to the past and future of African Americans?

d. In what ways can Ecclesiastes 11 be applied to the Black church in America today?

e. In what ways can Isaiah 30:19-26 be applied to the future of Black people throughout the Diaspora?

f. SUMMARY QUESTION: Compile a list of warnings and promises contained in the Scriptures listed in a-e. How can African American church leaders use them in formulating plans for revitalizing African American communities?

2. Understanding

In the Parable of the Source, our Lord mentions that there is a real danger in hearing the word of God but not taking the time to acquire an understanding of it.

a. What is the source of understanding and how can understanding affect one's life? (Proverbs 2:1-8)

b. In what ways can wisdom and understanding affect community life? (Proverbs 3:13-35)

c. Compare and contrast the ultimate outcome of the life of the foolish with that of the righteous. What does understanding have to do with it? (Proverbs 4:1-9; 14:7-9)

d. Where should a person go to make contact with wisdom and gain understanding? Make a list of possible sources. (Proverbs 8)

e. Compare and contrast stupid people with wise people. What does understanding have to do with it? (Proverbs 9)

f. SUMMARY QUESTION: If you were writing a one–paragraph letter to a young African American male entering high school for the first time, how could you use the contents of these proverbs to guide him?

3. Tribulation and Persecution

In the Parable of the Sower, our Lord mentions people who shy away from obedience to God, because of threats of tribulation or persecution.

a. What effect can the study of Black history have on Africans throughout the Diaspora? (Deuteronomy 4:27-40)

b. What is the source of hope in the midst of trouble? (Romans 5:1-6)

c. Does the presence of trouble mean that God has abandoned Black people living in politically oppressive countries? Explain. (Romans 8:35-39)

d. What message does the following passage carry for the "me first" generation? (Romans 12:1-13)

e. Is it enough for African American Christians to have understanding and wisdom among themselves? Explain. (2 Timothy 3:12—4:5)

f. SUMMARY QUESTION: If you were preparing a Bible study devotional for Black people in South Africa, list five topics, based on the Scriptures listed, that would be good for meditation.

4. The Love of Riches

In the Parable of the Sower, our Lord warns against the love of riches.

a. What are some advantages in applying the African principle of Ujima (collective work and responsibility), rather than the American principle of "rugged individualism"? (Ecclesiastes 4:4-12)

b. Explain the phrase, "money isn't everything." (Ecclesiastes 9:11-18)

c. Is the state of being rich in itself a curse? Explain. (1 Timothy 6:17-19; Mark 10:23, 24)

d. Some people feel that the amount of money one has indicates the quality of his/her spiritual life. Is this true? Explain. (Proverbs 11:1-7; 27:23-24)

e. Compare and contrast evil men who trust in riches with good men who trust in God. In what ways will they experience death and the afterlife differently? (Psalm 49)

f. SUMMARY QUESTION: Throughout the Diaspora and across the continent of Africa, oppressors exploit poor Black people to gain wealth. In at least one of the Scriptures in a-e, identify at least one strategy which Africans throughout the world can use to begin planning how to deal with this situation.

5. Fruit

In the Parable of the Sower, our Lord says that people who understand the Word of God will bear the "fruit" of love.

a. The fruit of the Spirit can result in a realization of the African principle, Umoja (unity). How does this work?

228

(Galatians 5:16-26; Ephesians 4:16)

b. In what way can the fruit of the Spirit (love) result in the African principle of Ujima (collective work and responsibility)? (John 15:1-17; Acts 2:42-47)

c. What is one way the fruit of the Spirit can result in the African principle of Ujamaa (cooperative economics)? (Luke 3:7-14; Acts 4:32-35)

d. What is another way that the fruit of the Spirit can result in Ujamaa? (Leviticus 23:17-22; Malachi 3:8-12; Acts 6:1-10)

e. How can the fruit of the Spirit result in the African principle of Kujichagulia (self-determination)? (Joshua 6:1-4, 15-21; Ephesians 6:10-18)

f. SUMMARY QUESTION: Based on your answers, is a relationship with God merely an "opiate of the people," or can it have practical "this worldly" consequences? Explain.

6. CHURCH-BASED MINISTRY

Based partially on your answers to the previous five exercises, present an argument for your church's missionary society and/or outreach program establishing some form of communication with Black people in other countries. Practically speaking, what is one specific manner in which this objective could be achieved?

7. PERSONAL APPLICATION

Is there a way in which you can make a personal contribution to the life of a person (or groups of people) in another country? You might give special consideration to children of African descent in other countries. If so, begin praying about your contribution now. In what ways might Africans in other countries enrich your life in return?

FOOTNOTES

Introduction

1. Basil Davidson, *The African Slave Trade* (Boston: Little Brown, 1980), p. 32.

2. Maulana Karenza, *Introduction to Black Studies* (Los Angeles: University of Sanrose Press, 1989), p. 109.

3. Charles Sims, *The Religious Education of Southern Negroes* (Louisville: Scripture Press Foundation, Christian Education Research Division, 1926), p. 97.

4. United States Center for Health Statistics, *Vital Statistics of the United States*, annual and unpublished data and U.S. Bureau of the Census 1990, *Current Population Statistics,* series P-25, No. 108.

5. United States Department of Commerce. Bureau of the Census. *The Black Population of the United States*, March 1990, p. 4.

6. *Chicago Defender,* Vol. LXXXV1, No. 195, February 8, 1992, p. 1.

7. United States Department of Justice, *Criminal Victimization in the United States,* Pediatric Trauma Registry NID, (Washington: June 1989), p. 42.

8. *National Center for Health Statistics,* 1988 report.

9. *Soucebook of Criminal Justice* (New York: New York Times, 1989), p. 261.

10. George Gallup, *The Gallup Report,* Report No. 265 (Princeton: Gallup Organization, October 1987), p. 43.

11. Milton J. Yinger, *Black Americans and Predominantly White Churches* (Washington: Committee on the Status of Black Americans, National Research Council, 1989), and C. Kirk Hadaway, David G. Hackett and James Miller, *Review of Religious Research* No. 25, March, 1989, p. 204-219.

12. Eric Lincoln and Lawrence Mamiya, *The Black Church in the African American Experience* (Durham: Duke University Press, 1990), p. 57.

13. *Ibid.,* p. 141.

14. Colleen Birchett, "Results of the Urban Ministries Needs Assessment," *Urban Religious Education,* edited by Donald Rogers (Nashville: Religious Education Press, 1989), p. 103.

15. *Op. Cit.,* Lincoln and Mamiya, p. 148-151.

16. *Op. Cit.,* Lincoln and Mamiya, p. 148-151.

17. *Op. Cit.,* Lincoln and Mamiya, p. 136.

The African Presence in Scripture

1. *New York Times,* February 21, 1989, p. 2A.

2. *Ibid.*

3. C. Eric Lincoln and Lawrence A. Mamiya, *The Black Church in the African American Experience* (Durham: Duke University Press, 1990), p. 388-391.

4. Walter A. McCray, *The Black Presence in the Bible* (Chicago: Black Light Fellowship, 1990), p. 92.

5. John Johnson, *The Black Biblical Heritage* (Nashville: Winston-Derek Publishers, 1991), p. 35.

6. *Ibid.,* p. 67.

7. Ivan Van Sertima, *Blacks in Science: Ancient and Modern* (New Brunswick: Transaction Publishers, 1988), p. 215.

8. *Ibid.,* p. 103.

9. Richard Green, *A Salute to Black Scientists and Inventors* (Chicago: Empak Publishers, 1989), p. 7.

10. George James, *Stolen Legacy* (New York: Philosophical Library, 1954), p. 73.

11. *Op. Cit.,* Van Sertima, p. 93.

12. *Op. Cit.,* James, p. 123.

13. *Op. Cit.,* Van Sertima, p. 30.

14. *Op. Cit.,* Johnson, p. 20.

15. *Newsweek,* January 11, 1988, p. 46.

16. *Op. Cit.,* McCray, p. 30.

17. *Op. Cit.,* McCray, p. 32.

18. Cain Hope Felder, *Troubling Biblical Waters* (Maryknoll: Orbis Books, 1989), p. 80.

19. *Op. Cit.,* Johnson, p. 103.

20. *Op. Cit.,* Johnson, p. 103.

21. *Op. Cit.,* McCray, p. 125.

22. *Op. Cit.,* McCray, p. 75.

In Need of a Miracle

1. Bureau of Labor Statistics, "Employment Situation: January, 1990," News Release, Table A-3.

2. Bureau of Labor Statistics, "Employment Situation: November 1990," News Release, Table A-3.

3. United States Department of Commerce, Bureau of the Census, "Money Income and Poverty Status: 1989," Tables 19, 20, and 21.

4. United States Department of Commerce, Bureau of the Census, "Money Income and Poverty Status in the United States: 1989," Table 8.

5. United States Department of Commerce, Bureau of the Census, "The Black Population of the United States: March 1990." News Release.

A Word About Addictions

1. New York Times/CBS News Poll, 1986, *Sourcebook of Criminal Statistics,* 1988, 1989, p. 261.

2. Gerald May, *Addiction and Grace* (New York: Harper & Rowe, 1988,) p. 32.

Genocide, Survival, or Victory?

1. Milton J. Yinger, *Black Americans and Predominantly White Churches* (Washington: Committee on the Status of Black Americans, National Research Council, 1989), and C. Kirk Hadaway, David G. Hackett and James Miller, *Review of Religious Research,* No. 25, March 1989, pg. 204-219.

2. Eric Lincoln and Lawrence H. Mamiya, *The Black Church in The African American Experience* (Durham: Duke University Press, 1990), p. 388-391.

The African American Male

1. United States Bureau of the Census, Current Population Reports, Series, 1990, p-25, No. 108.

2. National Center for Health Statistics. March 14, News Release, 1990.

3. *Chicago Defender,* Vol. LXXXV1, No. 194, February 8, 1992, p. 1.

4. United States Department of Justice, *Criminal Victimization in the United States* (Washington: NC J-115-524), June 1989, p. 42.

5. *Ibid.*

6. Statistical Abstracts, "State Prison Inmates, by Criminal History and Selected Characteristics of the Inmate: 1986," and United States Bureau of Justice Statistics, "Profile of State Prison Inmates," 1986, January 1988.

7. Center for Disease Control, News Release, May 16, 1991.

8. Center for Disease Control, News Release, December, 1990.

9. Eric Lincoln and Lawrence Mamiya, *The Black Church in the African American Experience* (Durham: Duke University Press, 1990), p. 109.

Preparing the Next Generation

1. American Council on Education, News Release, January 20, 1991.

2. United States Department Commerce. Bureau of the Census. *The Black Population of the United States,* March 1990.

3. *Ibid.,* Table 1, p. 17 and Figure 10; and U.S. Department of Commerce, Bureau of the Census, *Money Income and Poverty Status*: 1989, Tables 19, 20 and 21.

4. United States Department of Labor, News Release, May 1991.

5. National Center for Health Statistics, News Release, March 14, 1991.

6. George Gallup, Jr., *The Gallup Report,* Report No. 265 (Princeton: The Gallup Poll, October 1987), p. 43.

7. Eric Lincoln and Lawrence Mamiya, *The Black Church in the African American Experience* (Durham: Duke University Press, 1990), pp. 326-328.

8. Bennie Goodwin, *Helping Youth Grow* (Atlanta: Goodpatrick, 1980), p. 5.

9. J. O. Brubaker and R. E. Clark, *Understanding People* (Wheaton, Illinois: ETTA), p. 3.

10. Dave Wilkerson, *The Cross and the Switchblade* (New York: Jove, 1977).

11. Malcolm X, *The Autobiography of Malcolm X* with the assistance of Alex Haley, (New York: Grove Press, 1964).

12. Tom Skinner, *Black and Free* (Grand Rapids: Zondervan, 1977).

13. See Joy Mackay, *Creative Camping* (Wheaton, Illinois: Victor Books, 1977). In addition to the various denominational youth conferences and conventions, an annual youth meeting worth exploring is the Interdenominational Teen Conference. It meets each July in or near a major city in the United States and focuses all of its programs and activities around Black teens; For information write to Mrs. Elizabeth Howard, 23895 Rockingham, Southfield, Michigan, 48034. Senator Cleo Fields, youngest State Senator from Louisiana and Miss America, 1988. Dr. Debbye Turner are two of Teen Conferences' recent inspirational speakers.

See also Bennie Goodwin, *Helping Youth Grow* pp. 6-16. See also Bennie Goodwin, *The Effective Black Church* (Atlanta: Goodpatrick, 1990) pp. 18-19.

14. See Moseley, *Loc. Cit.*

15. See Bennie Goodwin, *The Efective Leader* (Atlanta: Goodpatrick, edition, 1989), pp. 8, 41-45. For four examples of models of Black community leadership see Robert Franklin's *Liberating Visions,* (Minneapolis: Fortress, 1990).

Church Conflicts

1. Eric Lincoln and Lawrence Mamiya, *The Black Church in the African American Experience* (Durham: Duke University Press, 1990), p. 145.

2. *Ibid.,* p. 148-151

3. *Ibid.,* p. 326

4. *Ibid.,* p. 141

5. *Ibid.,* p. 326

6. *Ibid.,* p. 327

Forgiving, Unifying and Strategizing

1. United States Department of Commerce, Bureau of the Census. *The Black Population of the United States,* March 1990, p. 17.

2. *Op. Cit.,* Lincoln and Mamiya, pp. 151-155.

3. *Op. Cit.,* Lincoln and Mamiya, p. 148.

4. *Op. Cit.,* Lincoln and Mamiya, p. 136.

5. *Op. Cit.,* Lincoln and Mamiya, p. 225.

The Church in the Community

1. *Op. Cit.,* Lincoln and Mamiya, p. 141.

2. Deiderick Bonhoffer, *The Martyred Christian* (New York: McMillan Press, 1985), p. 4.

3. Eric Lincoln and Lawrence Mamiya, *The Black Church in the African American Experience* (Durham: Duke University Press, 1990), p. 326.

Winning People

1. Eric Lincoln and Lawrence Mamiya, *The Black Church in the African American Experience* (Durham: Duke University Press, 1990), p. 141.

Facing the 21st Century

1. Colleen Birchett, *Results of the Urban Ministries Needs Assessment in Urban Church Education* Edited by Don Rogers (Nashville: Religious Education Press, 1989), p. 105.

2. Children's Defense Fund, *The State of America's Children* (Washington: The Fund, 1991), p. 2.

3. Carter G. Woodson, *The History of the Negro Church* (Washington: Associated Publishers, 1945), p. 20.

4. T. B. Boyd, III, *The New National Baptist Hymnal* (Nashville: National Baptist Publishing Board, 1977), p. 504.

5. John Johnson, *Succeeding Against the Odds* (New York: Warner Books, 1989), p. 50.

6. Bart Landry, *The New Black Middle Class* (Berkeley: University of California Press, 1987), p. 40.

7. Julius Wilson Williams, *The Truly Disadvantaged* (Chicago: University of Chicago Press, 1987).

8. Andrew Billingsley, *Children of the Storm* (New York: Haucourt Brace Jovanovich, 1972).

9. *Chicago Tribune,* October 13, 1991, p. 1.

10. Benjamin Mays and Joseph William Nicholson, *The Negro's Church* (New York: Arnold Press, 1933), p. 50.

Sowing Seeds in the Diaspora

1. Eric Lincoln and Lawrence Mamiya, *The Black Church in the African American Experience* (Durham: Duke University Press, 1990), p. 148.

2. Colleen Birchett, *Results of the Urban Ministries Needs Assessment in Urban Church Education* Edited by Donald Rogers, (Nashville: Religious Education Press, 1989), p. 105.

3. Shawna Moore, *The African Presence in the Americans* (Miami: Florida International University, Conference of Negritude, Race and Ethnicity in the Americas, 1987).

4. Chester Himes, *The Collected Stories of Chester Himes* (New York: Thundees' Mouth Press, 1991). p. 52.

5. Henry McNeal Turner, *Respect Black: The Writings and Speeches of Henry McNeal Turner* (New York: Arno Press, 1971), p. 103.

6. Edward Wilmot Bryden, *Selected Works of Dr. Edward Wilmot Bryden* (Liberia: Tubman Center of African Culture, 1976), p. 52.

7. Gerda Lerner, *Black Women in White America: A Documentary History* (New York: Pantheon Books, 1972), p. 82.

8. Carter G. Woodson, *The Miseducation of the Negro* (New York: AMS Press, 1977), p. 20.

9. Alexander Crummel, *Africa and America: Addresses and Decisions of Alexander Crummel* (Springfield, Mass: Wiley & Co., 1981), p. 301.

10. Toni Cade Bambara, *Tales and Stories for Black Folk* (Garden City: Zenith Books, 1971), p. 32.

11. *Op. Cit.,* Crummel, p. 303.

BIBLIOGRAPHY

Abatso, George, and Yvonne. *How to Equip the African American Family.* Edited by Colleen Birchett. Chicago: Urban Ministries, Inc., 1991.

Alexander, John F. "The State of the Black Movement." *Other Side.* No. 93, p. 5-54, June 1979.

Alexander, Walters A. *This Worldly Mission: The Life and Career of Alexander Walters.* New York: State University of New York at Stony, 1984. Dissertation Abstracts International, Volume 45/05-A, p. 1490, Order No. AA 84-16628.

Allen, Doyle R. *A Study of the Nature and Mission of the Black Church: With Emphasis on Preaching in the Black Methodist Church.* Perkins School of Theology.

Allen, Georgia. *The Black Church and Its Ministry to the Disadvantaged: With Emphasis on Preaching.* Perkins School of Theology, 1985.

Alvis, Joel Lawrence. *The Bounds of Their Habitations: The Southern Presbyterian Church, Racial Ideology and the Civil Rights Movement, 1946-1972.* Auburn University 1985. Dissertation Abstracts International, Volume 46/06-A, p. 1717, Order No. AAD85-18402.

Anderson, Talmadge. "Economic Dimensions of the Black Church: Managerial and Financial Strategies for Survival and Development." *Journal of the Interdenominational Theological Center,* Volume 13, No. 1, p. 39-54, Fall 1985.

Armstrong, Thomas F. "The Building of a Black Church Community in Post Civil War Liberty County." *Georgia Historical Quarterly.* Volume 66, No. 3, p. 346-367.

Augman, William Joseph, Jr. *The Black Church in America: An Exploration in Cincinnati.* Drew University, 1983. Dissertation Abstracts International, Volume 44/11-A, p. 3410, Order No. AAD84-04021.

Baldwin, Lewis, V. "Black Women and African Methodism, 1813-1983." *Meth H,* Volume 21, p. 225-237, July 1983.

_____. "Martin Luther King, Jr., The Black Church, and the Black Messianic Vision." *Journal of the Interdenominational Theological Center,* Volume 12, p. 93-108, Fall, 1984 - Spring, 1985.

Banks, Melvin, E. *Winning and Keeping Teens in the Church.* Chicago: Urban Ministries, Inc., 1975.

Becker, William H. "The Black Church: Manhood and Mission." *Journal of the American Academy of Religion,* Volume 40, No. 3, p. 316-333, 1972.

Bennett, Gerald Graham. *The Black Church in American Culture: An Empirical Study of Black Church Members' Perception of the Black Church in Albany, Georgia as a Social Change Agent.* Bowling Green State University, 1982. Dissertations Abstract International, Volume 44101-A, p. 284.

Birchett, Colleen. "A History of Religious Education in the Black Church." *Urban Church Education.* Edited by Donald B. Rogers. Birmingham: Religious Education Press, 1989.

_____. "African Americans." *Christian Education: Foundations for the Future.* Edited by Robert E. Clark, Lin Johnson, and Allyn K. Sloat. Chicago: Moody Press, 1991.

_____. "Black Teens and the AIDS Crisis." *INTEEN TEACHER,* Volume 10, No. 3, June, July, August, 1991, p. A.

_____. "Countering Street Culture." *INTEEN TEACHER,* Volume 7, No. 4, September, October, November, 1988, p. A.

_____. "Developing Leadership Skills Through Experience." *INTEEN TEACHER,* Volume 7, No. 2, March, April, May 1988, p. A.

_____. *How to Equip the African American Family: Leader's Guide.* Chicago: Urban Ministries, Inc., 1991.

_____. *How to Help Hurting People.* Chicago: Urban Ministries, Inc., 1990.

_____. *How to Help Hurting People: Leader's Guide.* Chicago: Urban Ministries, Inc., 1990.

_____. *IMANI NGUZO SZABA CURRICULUM.* Chicago: Trinity United Church of Christ, 1990.

_____. *INTEEN.* Chicago: Urban Ministries, Inc., 1986 - present.

_____. *KUUMBA NGUZO SZABA CURRICULUM.* Chicago: Trinity United Church of Christ, 1989.

_____. *NIA NGUZO SZABA CURRICULUM.* Chicago: Trinity United Church of Christ, 1991.

_____. "Rescuing the Young Black Male." *INTEEN TEACHER,* Volume 8, No. 2, March, April, May 1989, p. A.

_____. "Rome in Africa at the Time of the Apostle Paul." *INTEEN TEACHER,* Volume 10, No. 4, September, October, November, 1991, p. A.

_____. "Teen Challenge: For Young Drug Addicts." *INTEEN TEACHER,* Volume 8, No. 3, June, July, August 1989, p. A.

_____. "Using Case Studies With Teens." *INTEEN TEACHER,* Volume 9, No. 3, June, July, August 1990, p. A.

_____. "Using the Case Study Method with Adults." *How to Pray and Communicate with God,* by Dr. Walter Banks, edited with Case Study Applications by Dr. Colleen Birchett. Chicago: Urban Ministries, 1988, p. 5.

Boesack, Allan A. "The Black Church and the Future in South Africa." *Conflicting Ways of Interpreting the Bible.* Edited by H. Kung, p. 47-54, 1980.

Bradley, Michael R. "The Role of the Black Church in the Colonial Slave Society." *Louisiana Studies,* Volume 14, No. 4, 1975, p. 413-421.

Bray, Hiawatha. "A Separate Altar: Distinctives of the Black Church." *CHR T,* Volume 30, No. 13, p. 21-23, September 19, 1986.

Brubaker, J. O and Clark, Robert. *Understanding People.* Wheaton, Illinois: Evangelical Teacher Training Association, 1981.

Bruce, Robert. *A Black Church: Ecstacy in a World of Trouble.* Washington University, 1970. Dissertation Abstracts International, Volume 31/07-A, p. 3675.

Bryant, John R. *The Black Church as Hub of a Black National Community.* Colgate Rochester Divinity School, Crozer Theological Seminary, 1978. Dissertation Abstracts International, Volume X1978.

Burke, Cyril. *Venture in Mission: St. Monica's Episcopal Church, A Middle Class Predominantly Black Church Attempts to Minister to Its Community.* The Hartford Seminary Foundation, 1982.

Butler, Jon. "Communities and Congregations: The Black Church in St. Paul 1860-1900." *Journal of Negro History,* Volume 56, No. 2, 1971, p. 118-134.

Carruthers, Iva. "Africanity and the Black Woman." *Black Books Bulletin.* Volume 6, No., p. 14-20, 71.

Carruthers, Jacob, and Maulana Karenga. *Kemet and the African Worldview.* Los Angeles: University of Sankore Press, 1986.

Cartwright, John H. "The Black Church and the Call for Peace." Drew G., Volume 54, No. 1, p. 49-59, 1983.

Chavis, Benjamin F. "Liberation Theology and the Black Church." *CRJ Reporter,* p. 36-40, Summer 1980.

Clark, Reginald. *Family Life and School Achievement: Why Poor Black Children Succeed or Fail.* Chicago, Illinois: The University of Chicago Press, 1983.

Clarke, John Henrik. *African World Revolution.* Trenton: Africa World Press, 1991.

Cone, James. "Black Consciousness and the Black Church: A Historical-Theological Interpretation." *The Annals of the American Academy of*

Political and Social Science, January, 1970, p. 387.

Cone, James. "Martin Luther King, Jr., Black Theology – Black Church." *Theology Today,* Volume 40, p. 409-420, January 1984.

Cooper, Nicholas and Mitchell, Henry. *Soul Theology: The Heart of American Black Culture.* San Franciso: Harper and Row, 1986.

Copher, Charles. "Blacks and Jews in Historical Interaction." *African Presence in Early Asia.* Edited by Ivan Van Sertima and Runoko Rashidi. Transaction Publishers: 1988.

Crafford, Dionne. "The Ecumene in Africa." *Missionalia,* Volume 8, No. 1, p. 3-16, April, 1980.

Daniel, Jack L. and Geneva Smitherman. "How I Got Over: Communication Dynamics in the Black Community." *Quarterly Journal of Speech,* Volume 62, No. 1, 1976, p. 26-39.

D'Antonio, William V. and Joan Aldous (eds.) *Families and Religions: Conflict and Change in Modern Society.* Beverly Hills: Sage Publications, 1983, p. 320.

Del Pino, Julius E. "The Black Church in the '80s: A Call to Rebellion and the Cross." *Witness,* Volume 64, p. 12-14, September, 1981.

Dennis, Ruth E. "Social Stress and Mortality among Nonwhite Males." *Phylon,* Volume 38, No. 3, September 1977, p. 315-328.

Dickerson, Dennis C. "The Black Church in Industrializing Western Pennsylvania, 1870-1950." *Western Pennsylvania Historical Magazine,* Volume 64, No. 4, 1981, p. 329-344.

Diop, Cheikh Anta. *The African Origin of Civilization: Myth or Reality.* Chicago: Lawrence Hill Books, 1975.

_____. *Civilization or Barbarism: An Authentic Anthropology.* Brooklyn: Lawrence Hill Books, 1991.

_____. *The Cultural Unity of Black Africa.* London: Karnak House, 1989.

_____. *Precolonial Black Africa.* Brooklyn: Lawrence Hill Books, 1987.

Douglas, Robert Christy. *Power, Its Locus and Function in Defining Social Commentary in the Church of Christ, A Case Study of Black Civil Rights.* University of Southern California, 1980. Dissertation Abstracts International, Volume 42/01-A, p. 255.

Eakin, Sue Lyles. *The Black Struggle for Education in Louisiana, 1877-1930s.* University of Southwestern Louisiana, 1980. Dissertation Abstracts International, Volume 41/09-A, p. 4132, ORDER NO. AAD81-00 288.

Edwards, Herbert O. "A Call to Covenant, Black Churches and the Community: The Electronic Church." *AME Zion Quarterly Review,* Volume 96, No. 1, p. 13-28, April, 1984.

Eng, Eugenia, John Hatch and Anne Callan. "Institutionalizing Social Support Through Church and into the Community." *Health Education Quarterly,* Volume 12, No. 1, Spring, 1985, p. 81-91.

Evans, James H. Jr. "Keepers of the Dream: The Black Church and Martin Luther King, Jr." *American Baptist Quarterly,* Volume 5, No. 1, p. 75-84, March, 1986.

Feagan, Joe R. "The Black Church: Inspiration or Opiate?" *Journal of Negro History,* Volume 60, No. 4, p. 536-540, 1975.

Felder, Cain H. "The Usage of the Bible within American Black Churches." *AME Zion Quarterly Review,* Volume 95, No. 4, p. 2-10, January 1984.

_____. *Troubling Biblical Waters.* Maryknoll: Orbis Books, 1989.

Felton, Carroll M. *The Care of Souls in the Black Church.* Colgate Rochester Divinity School: Bexley Hall/Crozer Theological Seminary, 1975. Dissertation Abstracts International, Volume X1978.

Foster, Charles, et. al. *Christian Education Journey of Black Americans.* Nashville: Discipleship Resources, 1985.

Foster, Charles and Shockley, editors. *Working With Black Youth* Nashville: Abingdon, 1989.

Franklin, Robert. *Liberting Visions.* Minneapolis: Fortress, 1990.

Garrelts, George. "Black Power and Black Liturgy." *Journal of Religious Thought,* Volume 39, p. 34-45, Spring-Summer, 1982.

Gilkes, Cheryl Townsend. "The Black Church as a Therapeutic Community: Suggested Areas for Research into the Black Religious Experience." *Journal of the Interdenominational Theological Center,* Volume 8, p. 29-44, Fall, 1980.

Gillespie, Bonnie J. "The Black Church and the Black Elderly: A Bibliographical Historical Essay." *Journal of Stubenville, Ohio,* Volume 10, No. 2, p. 19-31, 1983.

Goba, Bonganjalo. "Doing Theology in South Africa: A Black Christian Perspective: An Invitation to the Church to Be Relevant." *Journal of Theology of South Africa,* No. 31, p. 23-35, June 1980.

_____. "The Roles of the Black Church in the Process of Healing Human Brokenness: A Perspective in Pastoral Theology." *Journal of Theology of South Africa,* No. 28, p. 7-13, September 1979.

Goodwin, Bennie, E. *Beside Still Waters.* Atlanta: Goodpatrick Publishers, 1973.

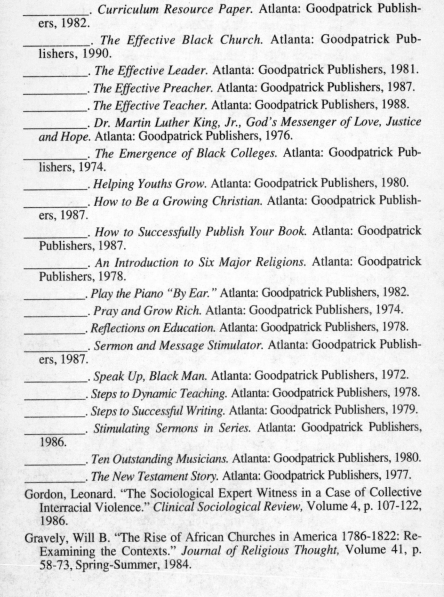

_____. *Curriculum Resource Paper*. Atlanta: Goodpatrick Publishers, 1982.

_____. *The Effective Black Church*. Atlanta: Goodpatrick Publishers, 1990.

_____. *The Effective Leader*. Atlanta: Goodpatrick Publishers, 1981.

_____. *The Effective Preacher*. Atlanta: Goodpatrick Publishers, 1987.

_____. *The Effective Teacher*. Atlanta: Goodpatrick Publishers, 1988.

_____. *Dr. Martin Luther King, Jr., God's Messenger of Love, Justice and Hope*. Atlanta: Goodpatrick Publishers, 1976.

_____. *The Emergence of Black Colleges*. Atlanta: Goodpatrick Publishers, 1974.

_____. *Helping Youths Grow*. Atlanta: Goodpatrick Publishers, 1980.

_____. *How to Be a Growing Christian*. Atlanta: Goodpatrick Publishers, 1987.

_____. *How to Successfully Publish Your Book*. Atlanta: Goodpatrick Publishers, 1987.

_____. *An Introduction to Six Major Religions*. Atlanta: Goodpatrick Publishers, 1978.

_____. *Play the Piano "By Ear."* Atlanta: Goodpatrick Publishers, 1982.

_____. *Pray and Grow Rich*. Atlanta: Goodpatrick Publishers, 1974.

_____. *Reflections on Education*. Atlanta: Goodpatrick Publishers, 1978.

_____. *Sermon and Message Stimulator*. Atlanta: Goodpatrick Publishers, 1987.

_____. *Speak Up, Black Man*. Atlanta: Goodpatrick Publishers, 1972.

_____. *Steps to Dynamic Teaching*. Atlanta: Goodpatrick Publishers, 1978.

_____. *Steps to Successful Writing*. Atlanta: Goodpatrick Publishers, 1979.

_____. *Stimulating Sermons in Series*. Atlanta: Goodpatrick Publishers, 1986.

_____. *Ten Outstanding Musicians*. Atlanta: Goodpatrick Publishers, 1980.

_____. *The New Testament Story*. Atlanta: Goodpatrick Publishers, 1977.

Gordon, Leonard. "The Sociological Expert Witness in a Case of Collective Interracial Violence." *Clinical Sociological Review*, Volume 4, p. 107-122, 1986.

Gravely, Will B. "The Rise of African Churches in America 1786-1822: Re-Examining the Contexts." *Journal of Religious Thought*, Volume 41, p. 58-73, Spring-Summer, 1984.

Gray, Cleo Jones. *Attitudes of Black Church Members Toward the Black Elderly as a Function of Denomination, Age, Sex, and Level of Education.* Howard University: Washington, D.C., 1977. Dissertation Abstract International, Volume 38/11-A, p. 6396, ORDER NO. AAD78-05 433.

Green, Garey. *The Black Church and the Criminal Justice System: A Pilot Project Designed to Train Black Clergy and Laymen in Pastoral Care and Counseling.* Lutheran Theological Southern Seminary, 1982.

Green, Roosevelt. *A Functional Analysis of the Black Church: Baptist Churches in Augusta, Georgia.* Pennsylvania State University, 1984. Dissertation Abstracts International, Volume 46/04-A, p. 1097.

Griffin, Ezra E. "The Impact of Culture and Religion on Psychiatric Care." *Journal of the National Medical Association,* Volume 74, No. 12, December, 1982.

Hale, Benson, Janice. *Black Children: Their Roots, Culture and Learning Styles.* Baltimore: John Hopkins University Press, 1986.

Hamilton, Charles Spencer. *The Black Church Ministry in Political Action in Augusta, Georgia.* Colgate Rochester Divinity School/Bexley Hall/Crozer Theological Seminary, 1975.

Hare, Nathan and Julia Hare. *Bringing the Black Boy to Manhood: the Passage.* San Francisco: The Black Think Tank, 1985.

Hargrove, Barbara, and Stephen, Jones. *Reaching Youth Today.* Valley Forge: Judson, 1983.

Harris, James Henry. *Laity Expectations of Ministers in the Black Church: A Study of Political and Social Expectations in the Context of Ministry to Community and World.* Old Dominion University, 1985. Dissertation Abstracts International, Volume 46/06-A, p. 1733.

Harris, Maria. *Portrait of Youth Ministry.* New York: Paulist Press, 1981.

Hayden, Robert, C. *Faith, Culture and Leadership: A History of the Black Church in Boston.* Boston: NAACP, 1983.

Henderson, Perry. *The Black Church Credit Union.* Lima: Fairway Press, 1990.

Henderson, Perry. *The Black Church Credit Union and the Management of Communal Financial Resources.* United Theological Seminary, 1986. Dissertation Abstracts International, Volume X1986.

Hodge, W. J. "The Black Church's Outreach." *The Black Church Experience,* Edited by Emmanual L. McCall, p. 73-84, 1972.

Hoekema, David A. "Black Churches, The Third World and Peace." *Christian Century,* Volume 100, p. 1100-1101, November 30, 1983.

245

Hood, Robert E. "The Role of Black Religion in Political Change: The Haitian Revolution and Voodoo (1791-1803)." *Journal of the Interdenominational Theological Center,* Volume 9, p. 45-69, Fall 1981.

Holderness, Ginny. *Youth Ministry.* Atlanta: Knox, 1981.

Hopkins, Dwight N. *Black Theology USA and South Africa: Politics, Culture, and Liberation.* Maryknoll: Orbis Books, 1990.

Houston, Drusilla Dunjee. *Wonderful Ethiopians of the Ancient Cushite Empire.* Baltimore: Black Classic Press, 1985.

Hunte, Christopher, and Cheryl A. Weber. *An Assessment of the Black Church's Role in Rural Development.* Southern University, Baton Rouge, Southern Association of Agricultural Scientists, Rural Sociology Section, Association Paper, 1985.

Hyman, Mark. *Blacks Who Died for Jesus.* Nashville: Winston-Derek Publishers, 1983.

Jackson, Jacquelyne Johnson. "Contemporary Relationships Between Black Families and Black Church the United States: A Speculative Inquiry." *Families and Religions.* Edited by W. D'Antonio and J. Aldous, p. 191-220, 1983.

Jackson, Jonathan. *Faith Journey Series, Sub-Sahara Africa and the Black American Church.* Geneva, 1984.

James, George. *Stolen Legacy.* New York: Philosophical Library, 1954.

Johnson, Dorothy. *A Guide for Youth in the A.M.E. Zion Church.* Greensboro: Johnson, 1985.

Johnson, John L. *The Black Biblical Heritage.* Nashville: Winston-Derek Publishers, 1991.

Johnson, Otis S. *Predictors of Social Action among Black Churches.* Savannah State College, Mid-South Sociological Association, 1977.

Johnson, Otis Samuel. *The Social Welfare Role of the Black Church.* Brandeis University, The F. Heller Graduate School for Advanced Studies in Social Welfare, 1980; Dissertation Abstracts International, Volume 41, ORDER NO. 5: 2293-A 8024554, p. 231.

Jones, Amos. *Paul's Message of Freedom: What Does It Mean to the Black Church?* Valley Forge: Judson Press, 1984.

Jones, Aubrey. *A Style of Ministry That Is Necessary for the Black Church in the Inner-City.* Eden Theological Seminary, 1976. Dissertation Abstracts International, Volume X1977.

Jones, Lawrence. "The Black Churches: A New Agenda?" *Christian Century,* Volume 96, p. 434, April 18, 1979.

_____. "Urban Black Churches: Conservators of Value and Sustainers of Community." *Journal of Religious Thought,* Volume 39, p. 41-50, Fall-Winter 1982-83.

Karenga, Maulana. *Introduction to Black Studies.* Los Angeles: University of Sankore Press, 1989.

Kearney, John Henry. *The Development of a Lay Ministry of Visitation to the Hospitalized and Shut-in Members of the Mount Calvary Missionary Baptist Church.* Drew University, 1982. Dissertation Abstracts International, Volume 43/09-A, p. 2950, ORDER NO. AAD83-0247.

Kiernan, James. "Themes and Trends in the Study of Black Religion in Southern Africa." *Journal of Religion in Africa,* Volume 12, No. 2, p. 136-147, 1981.

Kirkendoll, Chester A. "How did the Amsterdam Youth Conference of 1939 Affect the Black Church?" *Journal of Ecumenical Studies,* Volume 16, No. 1, 1979 p. 72-78.

Kotlowitz, Alex. *There Are No Children Here.* New York: Doubleday, 1991.

Kunjufu, Jawanza. *Countering the Conspiracy to Destroy Black Boys.* 2 vols. Chicago: African American Images, 1988.

_____. *Motivating and Preparing Black Youth to Work.* Chicago: African American Images, 1986.

_____. *To Be Popular or Smart: The Black Peer Group.* Chicago: African American Images, 1988.

Lawson, William B. "Chronic Mental Illness and the Black Family." *American Journal of Social Psychiatry,* Volume 6, No. 1, Winter, 1986, p. 57-61.

Levin, Jeffrey, S. "The Role of the Black Church in Community Medicine." *Journal of the National Medical Association,* Volume 76, No. 5, May, 1984, p. 477-483.

Lincoln, Eric, and Lawrence H. Mamiya. *The Black Church in the African American Experience.* Durham: Duke University Press, 1990.

Lincoln, Eric. "Martin Luther King, The Magnificent Intruder." *AME Zion Quarterly Review,* Volume 94, No. 2, p. 3-12, July 1982.

_____. "The Black Church in the American Society: A New Responsibility?" *Journal of the Interdenominational Theological Center,* Volume 6, p. 83-93, Spring, 1979.

Linsey, Nathaniel. "Black Church Union and Evangelism." *AME Zion Quarterly Review,* Volume 92, No. 4, p. 13-18, January 1981.

Little, Sara. *Youth, World and the Church.* Richmond: Knox, 1972.

Liu, Agnes Tat Fong. *The Contextual Fit of the Black Church to Certain Characteristics of the Poor (An Assessment Based on Survey of Literature and a Case Study)*. Fuller Theological Seminary of World Mission, 1985. Dissertation Abstracts International, Volume 46/05-A, p. 1306, ORDER NO. AAD85-13621.

Lloyd, Anthony Frazier. *The Urban Black Church's Role in Community Mental Health Care*. School of Theology at Claremont, 1985. Dissertation Abstracts International, Volume 46/06-A, p. 1650, ORDER NO. AAD85-16146.

Lovelace, Austin. *The Youth Choir*. Nashville: Abingdon Press, 1977.

Lyles, Michael R. and James Carter. "Myths and Strengths of the Black Family: A Historical and Sociological Contribution to Family Therapy." *Journal of the National Medical Association,* Volume 74, No 11, November 1982.

Mackay, Joy. *Creative Camping*. Wheaton: Victor Books, 1977.

Maier, Paul L. *Josephus: The Essential Writings*. Grand Rapids: Kregel Publications, 1988.

Marable, Manning. "The Black Faith of W.E.B. DuBois: Sociocultural and Political Dimensions of Black Religion." *The Southern Quarterly,* Volume 23, No. 3, Spring, 1985, p. 15-33.

Masamba, Jean, and Richard A. Kalish. "Death and Bereavement: the Role of the Black Church." *Omega: Journal of Death and Dying,* Volume 7, No. 1, 1976, p. 23-34.

Maxwell, Ashley Adolphus. *Growth-Group Dynamics and Holistic Ministry in the Afro-American Church*. Wesley Theological Seminary, 1986.

Mays, Joe H. *Black Americans and Their Contributions Toward Union Victory in the American Civil War*. Middle Tennessee State University, 1983. Dissertation Abstracts International, Volume 44/03-A, p. 835, ORDER NO. AAD83-17384.

McBeth, Leon. "Images of the Black Church In America." *Baptist History and Heritage,* Volume 16, No. 3, p. 19-28, 40, 1981.

McCall, Emmanuel. "The Black Church and Social Justice." *Issues in Christian Ethics*. Edited by P. Simmons, p. 197-212, 1980.

McCray, Walter. *The Black Presence in the Bible*. 2 vols. Chicago: Black Light Fellowship, 1990.

Millar, William R. "Racial Justice (Thematic Issue)." *American Baptist Quarterly*, Volume 5, No. 1, p. 1-84, March 1963.

Mitchell, Henry. "Towards a Black Evangelism." *Journal of Religious*

Thought, Volume 35, p. 55-67, Spring-Summer, 1978.

Mitchell, Mozella G. "Contemporary Issues and Implications for Women in Lay and Clergy Ministries in the Black Church of the Weslyan Tradition." *Wesleyan Theology Today,* p. 185-188, 1985.

Morris, Aldon Douglas. *The Rise of the Civil Rights Movement and Its Movement: Black Power, 1953-1963.* New York: State University of New York at Stony Brook, 1980.

Moyd, Olin. "Redemption in the Roots of Black Theology: A Model for the Evangelizing Community." *Foundations,* Volume 20, p. 306-317, October-December, 1977.

Mukenge, Ida Rousseau. *The Black Church in America: A Case Study in Political Economy.* University Press of America, Maryland, 1983.

Murphy, Larry George. "The Church and Black Californians: A Mid-nineteenth-Century Struggle for Civil Justice." *Foundations,* Volume 18, No. 2, 1975, p. 165-183.

Murray, Robert G. *The Black Alcoholic In and Out of the Black Church.* Boston University School of Theology, 1981.

Myers, William. *Black and White Styles of Youth Ministry (unpublished paper).* Chicago Theological Seminary, 1987.

Nelsen, Hart M., and Anne K. *Black Church in the Sixties.* University Press of Kentucky, 1975.

Nimmons, Julius Franklin Jr. *Social Reform and Moral Uplift in the Black Community, 1890-1910: Social Settlements, Temperance, and Social Purity.* Howard University, 1987. Dissertation Abstracts International, Volume 43/07-A, p. 2419, ORDER NO. AAD82-26720.

Onujiogu, Anne Amara. *Evaluation for the Workshop Teaching Method for Improving Sickle Cell Awareness Among Black Adults.* Boston University School of Education, 1981. Dissertation Abstracts International, Volume 41/12-A, p. 4687. ORDER NO. AAD81-12263.

Ortega, Suzanne T., Robert D. Crutchfield, and William A. Rushing. "Race Differences in Elderly Personal Well-Being: Friendship, Family and Church." *Research on Aging,* Volume 5, No. 1, March, 1983, p. 101-118.

Paris, Peter. "The Bible and the Black Churches." *The Bible and Social Reform.* Edited by E. Sandeen, p. 133-154, 1982.

_____. "The Moral and Political Significance of the Black Churches in America." *Belief and Ethics.* Edited by W. W. Schoreder, p. 315-329, 1978.

_____. *The Social Teaching of the Black Churches.* Philadelphia: Fortress Press, 1985.

_____. "The Social World of The Black Church." *Drew G.,* Volume 52, No. 3, p. 1-38, 1982.

Parker, Paige Alan. *Political Mobilization in the Rural South: A Case Study of Gadsden County, Florida.* University of Florida, 1980. Dissertation Abstracts International, Volume 41/06-A, p. 2752. ORDER NO. AAD80-29080.

Peck, Gary P. "Black Radical Consciousness and the Black Christian Experience: Toward a Critical Sociology of Afro-American Religion." *Social Analysis, Volume 43, p. 155-169, Summer 1982.*

Perkins, John. "A Vision for Service." *Other Side,* Volume 21, No. 7, p. 34-35, October 1985.

Perry, Lewis, and Michael Fellman. *Antislavery Reconsidered: New Perspectives on the Abolitionists.* Baton Rouge: Louisiana State University Press, 1979, p. 75-95.

Pope, Jacqueline. *Organizing Women on Welfare: Planning at the Grass Roots Level.* New York: Columbia University, 1986. Dissertation Abstracts International, Volume 47/03-A, p. 1080, ORDER NO. AAD86-10805.

Roberts, J. Deotis. "Impact of the Black Church: Sole Surviving Black Institution." *Journal of the Interdenominational Theological Center,* Volume 6, p. 138-147, Spring, 1979.

_____. *Roots of a Black Future: Family and Church.* Philadephia: Westminister Press, 1980.

Rodgers, Augustus, and Edward D. Hayes. "Development of a Counseling and Referral Service in a Black Church." *Psychiatric Forum,.* Volume 12, No. 2, Spring, 1984, p. 48-52.

Rodney, Walter. *How Europe Underdeveloped Africa.* Washington, D.C.: Howard University Press, 1982.

Rozzell, Liane. *"People of Color, People of Peace."* Conference, The Black Church, the Third World, and Peace, Atlanta, Georgia, Volume 13, No. 1, p. 8-9, January, 1984.

Sandeen, Ernest R. *The Bible and Social Reform.* Philadephia: Fortress Press, p. 184, 1982.

Sarfoh, Joseph A. "The West African Zongo and the American Ghetto: Some Comparative Aspects of the Roles of Religious Institutions." *Journal of Black Studies,* Volume 17, No. 1, September, 1986, p. 71-84.

Sawyer, Mary R. "A Moral Minority: Religious and Congressional Black Politics." *Journal of Religious Thought,* Volume 40, p. 55-66, Fall-Winter, 1983-84.

Shopshire, James M. "The Black Church and Economic Development: Past, Present, Future." *AME Zion Quarterly Review,* Volume 93, No. 1, p. 39-45, July 1981.

Shriver, Donald W. "The Churches and the Future of Racism." *Theology Today,* Volume 38, p. 142-159, July 1981.

_____. "Race, Americanism, and the Ministry of the Churches in the Eighties." *Journal of the Interdenominational Theological Seminary,* Volume 8, p. 111-117, Spring, 1981.

Simpkins, St. Julian. *Community Organization: A Strategy for Christian Mission in the Black Church.* Indiana University of Pennsylvania, 1978. Dissertation Abstracts Internatioanl, Volume 31/07-A, p. 3675.

Sindos, Louise King. *Services, Needs and Use Among a Population of Single Black Men and Women, Self-Help, Mutual Aid Group.* New York: City University of New York, 1986.

Smiley, Dolores, V. *The Relationship of a Belief System and Actual Performance Among Aged Black Individuals: The Collection of Data for a Longitudinal Study: Implications for Educators.* St. Louis University, 1985. Dissertation Abstracts International, Volume 47/01-A, p. 103, ORDER NO. AAD86-04415.

Smith, Archie, Jr. "An Interpretation of the People's Temple and Jonestown: Implications for The Black Church, Tables: Victims by Age, Sex, Race." *Journal of the Interdenominational Theological Center,* Volume 10, No. 1-2, p. 1-13, Fall-September 1982-83.

Smith, Jacqueline Marie. *Church Participation and Morale of the Rural, Southern Black Aged: The Effects of Socioeconomic Status, Gender and the Organizational Properties of Churches.* Ann Arbor: The University of Michigan, 1986.

Smith, Wallace Charles. *A Family Enrichment Curriculum for the Black Church.* Eastern Baptist Theological Seminary, 1979.

Smith, Wallace. *The Church in the Life of the Black Family.* Valley Forge: Judson Press, 1985.

Speaks, Ruben L. "The Role of the Black Church in the Building of A New Civilization." *AME Zion Quarterly Review,* Volume 93, No. 1, p. 4-11, April 1981.

Spivey, Charles S. "The Future of the Black Church." *CTS Register,* Volume 73, No. 1, pp. 49-54, Winter 1983.

Stewart, James B. *"Building a Cooperative Economy: Lessons from the Black Experience."* Review of Social Economy, Volume 42, No. 3, 1984, p. 360-368.

Strommen, Merton. *Five Cries of Youth.* New York: Harper and Row, 1974.

Stumme, Wayne C. *Christians and the Many Faces of Marxism.* Minneapolis: Augsburgh Press, 1984.

Tatum, Beverly Daniel. *Life in Isolation: Black Families Living in a Predominantly White Community.* Ann Arbor, Michigan: The University of Michigan, 1984. Dissertation Abstracts International, Volume 45/07-B, p. 2365, ORDER NO. AAD84-22337.

Thomas, Herman Edward. *An Analysis of the Life and Work of James W.C. Pennington, A Black Churchman and Abolitionist.* Hartford Seminary Foundation, 1978 Dissertation Abstracts International, Volume 43/03-A, p. 833.

Thomas, Lotta. *Biblical Faith and the Black American.* Valley Forge, Pa.: Judson Press, 1976.

Thomas, Robert. *Alternative Strategies for Inner City Black Churches in the Black Youth Job Crisis.* San Francisco Theological Seminary, 1973 Dissertation Abstracts International, Volume X 1973.

Tinney, James S. *A Theoretical and Historical Comparison of Black Political and Religious Movements.* Washington, D.C.: Howard University, 1978. Dissertation Abstracts International, Volume 41/10-A, p. 4471, ORDER NO. AAD81-06287.

Townes, Elmer. *Successful Biblical Youth Work.* Nashville: Impact, 1976.

Unger, Linda, and Kathleen Schultz. *Seeds of a People's Church: Challenge and Promise from the Underside of History.* Detroit: Neil C. McMath Lectures, 1980.

Van, Sertima, Ivan. and Runoko Rashidi. *African Presence in Early Asia.* New Brunswick: Transaction Publishers, 1988.

_____. *African Presence in Early Europe.* New Brunswick: Transaction Publishers, 1990.

_____. *Egypt Revisited.* New Brunswick: Transaction Publishers, 1991.

Vedlitz, Arnold, Jon P. Alston, and Carl Pinkele. "Politics and the Black Church in a Southern Community." *Journal of Black Studies,* Volume 10, No. 3, March, 1980, p. 367-375.

Vincent, John J. "Starting All Over Again: Hints of Jesus in the City." *Risk Book Series,* No. 13, p. 1-66, 1981.

Warren, Michael. *Youth, Gospel, Liberation.* New York: Harper and Row, 1987.

Wilmore, Gayraud S. *Black Religion and Black Radicalism.* Maryknoll: Orbis Books, 1990.

Williams, Chancellor. *The Destruction of Black Civilization.* Chicago: Third World Press, 1987.

Williams, Charles, Jr. "Contemporary Voluntary Associations in the Urban Black Church: The Development and Growth of Mutual Aid Societies." *Journal of Voluntary Action Research,* Volume 3, No. 4, October-December, 1984, p. 19-30.

Williams, Frederick. *The Black Church and the Politics of Futurism.* Colgate Rochester Divinity School: Crozer Theological Seminary, 1978. Dissertation Abstracts International, Volume X 1978.

Williams, James H. "Back to the Basics: A New Challenge for the Black Church." *Explorations in Ethnic Studies,* Volume 3, No. 1, p. 13-18, 1980.

Williams, Juan. *Eyes on the Prize: America's Civil Rights Years, 1954-1965.* New York: Penguin Books, 1987.

Wilmore, Gayraud. *Black Religion and Black Radicalism: Interpretation of Religious History of Afro-American People.* Maryknoll: Orbis Books, 1983.

Wilmore, Gayraud. "Tension Points in Black Church Studies." *Christian Century,* Volume 96, p. 411-413, April 11, 1976.

Wilson, Amos N. *The Developmental Psychology of the Black Child.* New York: Africana Research Publications, 1978.

Wimberly, Edward. "The Healing Tradition of the Black Church and Modern Science: A Model of Traditioning." *Journal of the Interdenominational Theological Center,* Volume 11, p. 19-30, Fall, 1983, Spring, 1984.

Woodson, Carter G. *The Miseducation of the Negro.* Nashville: Winston-Derek Publishers, 1990.

Woods, John Henry Jr. *The Black Church in the Ministry of Housing.* American Baptist Seminary of the West, 1981. Dissertation Abstracts International, Volume X1981.

Wright, Nathan. "Four Keys to Black Church Action." *St. Luke Journal,* Volume 22, p. 247-260.

Wyatt, Lawrence Paul. *Developing a Premarital Guidance Program Within a Group of Black Local Churches of God in the Detroit, Michigan Area.* Drew University, 1982. Dissertation Abstracts International, Volume 43/10-A, p. 3280, ORDER NO. AAD83-02426.

BIOGRAPHIES

Dr. Colleen Birchett is the editor of the series *How to Pray and Communicate with God, How to Help Hurting People, How to Equip the African American Family* and *Biblical Strategies for a Community in Crisis*. She is a development editor for Urban Ministries, Inc. in Chicago, Illinois.

Dr. Iva Carruthers is president of Nexus, Inc. and a professor at Northeastern Illinois University.

Dr. James Forbes is pastor of Riverside Church in New York.

Dr. Bennie E. Goodwin, II is senior editor at Urban Ministries, Inc. in Chicago, Illinois.

Crawford W. Loritts, Jr. is National Director of Legacy in Union City, Georgia. A ministry designed to help rebuild Black America's spiritual heritage.

Dr. William Pannell is a professor at Fuller Theological Seminary in Pasadena, California.

Tom Skinner is president of Skinner Evangelistic Associates in New York.

Dr. Kenneth B. Smith is president of Chicago Theological Seminary in Chicago, Illinois.

Dr. Hycel Taylor is pastor of Second Baptist Church in Evanston Illinois.

Dr. Clarence Walker is founder and president of Clarence Walker Ministries, and elder of the New Covenant Church of Philadelphia.

Dr. Jeremiah A. Wright, Jr. is pastor of Trinity United Church of Christ in Chicago, Illinois.